The Establishment Is Dead
The Rise and Election of Donald Trump

The Establishment Is Dead
The Rise and Election of Donald Trump

Ben Shapiro

Creators Publishing
Hermosa Beach, CA

Cover art by Peter Kaminski

CREATORS PUBLISHING
737 3rd St
Hermosa Beach, CA 90254
310-337-7003

ISBN (print): 978-1-945630-72-9
ISBN (ebook): 978-1-945630-73-6

First Edition
Printed in the United States of America
1   3   5   7   9   10   8   6   4   2

Contents

~~~

A Note From the Publisher

Since 1987, Creators has syndicated many of your favorite columns to newspapers. In this digital age, we are bringing collections of those columns to your fingertips. This will allow you to read and reread your favorite columnists, with your own personal digital archive of their work.

Creators Publishing

The Tearful Dictator

January 6, 2016

The tyrant cries.

While announcing his new slate of gun control measures designed to pave the way for a national gun registration regime, President Obama welled up in a press conference on Tuesday. He'd spent nearly half an hour berating Republicans, American voters and the National Rifle Association for their supposed intransigence in failing to embrace his executive actions. Finally, he reached up to his eyes, rubbed at them, and as tears wet his cheeks, he stated, "Every time I think about those kids, it gets me mad. ... We need voters who want safer gun laws, and who are disappointed in leaders who stand in their way, to remember come election time."

The American people, you see, have to change. They have to change because they are uncaring. And we know they are uncaring because the most powerful man on the planet weeps when he thinks of the little children.

But you don't, do you?

We've now reached the apex of the Feelings Age. It no longer matter what good policy looks like. It no longer matters what the Constitution says. All that matters is that our politicians care about people like us. During the 2012 election, Mitt Romney won a wide variety of exit polls regarding policy, from leadership skill to values. But he lost the election because Obama clocked him 81 percent to 18 percent on the crucial issue of "cares about people like me."

And now Obama has come to collect.

But he can't do it without the tears. That's because the tears grant him the patina of vulnerability. No one fears the dictator who shows his human side. We view those who violate our rights as nefarious members of an evil cabal, lurking in the night while cackling. We don't view them as highly attuned, sensitive people -- after all, the logic goes, if they were that sensitive, they'd stop before violating the rights of others.

Which is why crying is such an effective tactic for those who would violate your rights. Crying on behalf of victims puts you on the side of the angels, and your opponents on the side of the demons. And we don't tend to care what happens to demons. We're too busy rooting for the angels.

That's why President Obama followed up his lachrymose performance with a call to action against all of his enemies. It's why he talked at length about shredding the Second Amendment in favor of "other rights," as though my right to own a gun endangers your right to pursuit of life, liberty and happiness. It's why the media immediately leapt to cover Obama's waterworks instead of his policies -- because the story is Obama's emotional heroism and essential decency, not his absolute failure to find any real solution to gun violence.

So look for more Obama emotional blackmail. And look for more stories about Obama's emotional journey from the compliant press, which prints narratives about empathetic heroes -- even if those heroes are busy violating other people's rights at every turn.

The West's Terminal Radical Islam Denial Syndrome

January 13, 2016

Last year, there were 452 suicide terror attacks across the world. Four hundred and fifty of them were committed by Muslims. Last month, Muslims pledging allegiance to ISIS murdered 14 people in San Bernardino, California. Last week, thousands of Muslims around Europe, from Germany to Sweden to Switzerland, sexually assaulted hundreds of young women on New Year's Eve. Just days ago, a Muslim man shot a Philadelphia cop at point-blank range and declared that he did it in the name of Islam.

In response, Hillary Clinton declared, "Muslims are peaceful and tolerant people and have nothing whatsoever to do with Islam." She agreed this week that "white terrorism and extremism" are just as much a threat to Americans as ISIS and radical Islam, and then proceeded to blame "gun violence." The mayor of Cologne, Germany, told young women not to walk within "arm's length" of young Muslim men, and leftist commentators explained that the wave of sexual harassment resulted from some generalized, nonspecific religious patriarchal attitudes. The mayor of Philadelphia said that the attack on the police officer had nothing to do with "being a Muslim or the Islamic faith," and that instead, we ought to focus our attention on the pressing issue of gun violence: "There are just too many guns on the streets, and I think our national government needs to do something about that."

If the West keeps this up, there won't be any West of which to speak.

German chancellor Angela Merkel, who just won the Time magazine person of the year for her courageous decision to subject her citizens to the cultural sophistication of Muslims of non-Westernized Syrian Muslim refugees, is now preparing to allow another wave of such refugees into her country to enjoy New Year's Eve activities. According to Politico, Germany can expect another 1.5 million refugees this year, and according to Germany's minister for international development, "Eight to 10 million are still on their way."

Meanwhile, here at home, President Obama will invite a Syrian Muslim refugee to attend his State of the Union address so that he can browbeat Republicans about their supposed xenophobia with regard to the issue. The Syrian Muslim refugee entered the United States after a bombing killed seven family members; he's now living in Troy, Michigan. Obama wrote him a letter recently: "You're part of what makes America great." No word on whether Obama wrote letters to Palestinian Muslim refugees Omar Faraj Saeed Al Hardan, 24, of Houston, who was arrested last week for attempting to provide material support to ISIS, or Aws Mohammed Younis Al-Jayab, who was charged with making a false statement involving international terrorism, according to CNN.

Presumably, some people who don't make America great include Syrian Christian refugees, who have largely been excluded from the United States by the Obama administration. Simultaneously, ISIS happily continues to exploit the Radical Islam Denial Syndrome of the left; they've been planning a "sophisticated" smuggling operation to move people across the border into Turkey, from where refugees then enter the West.

The West is far too powerful to lose to ISIS or radical Islam -- unless the West decides to pretend that radical Islam doesn't exist. In pathological fashion, that's just what our leaders have apparently decided to do.

Donald Trump and the
Cult of Personality

January 20, 2016

"Power," Henry Kissinger once told The New York Times, "is the ultimate aphrodisiac." Kissinger might amend that statement today: Now, fame is power, and thus replaces power as the ultimate aphrodisiac. In fact, fame isn't just an aphrodisiac -- it's the ultimate nepenthe, a drug causing forgetfulness. The more famous our politicians are, the more we neglect their positions and character. No wonder the most admired woman in America is criminal Hillary Clinton, the most admired man is criminal Barack Obama, and the second-most admired man is loudmouth Donald Trump.

We assume that fame inoculates our politicians for the same reason we check Yelp reviews: If there are tons of people who recommend a restaurant, they can't all have been bribed. If tons of people like and support a politician, then, he or she must be worthwhile.

But this logic doesn't always work. If several people stand on a street corner and simultaneously look up in the air for no reason, passersby will begin staring up into the air, looking for the rationale behind the mass gaze. Our human desire for informational shortcuts -- our willingness to take another's word for it -- means that we end up looking like idiots when someone points out there's nothing up there.

Our media-reinforcing cycle of fame is more like a street corner of skyward-looking nincompoops than an aggregation of Yelp reviews. Our elites tell us that we ought to look at a given candidate in a given way; we then react to those elites by following their spotlight. Donald Trump has received nearly half of all media coverage in the Republican race since he announced his campaign. That means that a lot of people are willing to overlook his flubs and his foibles -- he's a known face, and that fame protects him from comments that would hurt any other candidate.

The problem here isn't Trump. It's our entire culture of politics. Barack Obama has made ubiquity an art form -- it's hard to imagine that someone who appears regularly with YouTube stars to talk about tampon taxes could actually be malignant. Joe Biden appears on "Parks and Recreation." Hillary Clinton dances with Ellen and makes awful jokes on "Saturday Night Live." Our politicians know that exposure makes us comfortable with them.

In truth, we should never be comfortable with our politicians. We should never trust them. Star worship of Ronald Reagan on the right leads establishment Republicans to idolize even his worst failures, like amnesty; star worship of Bill Clinton on the left leads Democrats to pooh-pooh his brutal treatment of women, and his wife's enabling of that behavior. Our celebrities have become royals, and our politicians have become celebrities.

That means we crown ourselves a king or queen every four years. And America needs no kings and queens. We need unimportant, decent people who focus on how to make themselves unimportant in our lives.

But that's not what we get. Instead, we get glitz and glamour, fun and frolicking with the people who control our freedoms. That's dangerous. We are dangerous, not Trump or even Obama or Hillary Clinton. Until we check our own impulse to blindly follow our celebrity political class, we shouldn't be surprised when our celebrities become politicians and our politicians become tyrants.

Anti-Establishment Does Not Mean Pro-Conservative

January 27, 2016

Donald Trump will change everything.

This seems to be the consensus among anti-establishment Republicans. According to the latest ABC News/Washington Post poll, Trump leads among anti-establishment primary voters with an actual majority of 51 percent. And a full 51 percent of Republicans think Trump is "the best choice to bring needed change to Washington, perhaps the single most crucial attribute to leaned Republicans."

Trump makes this case, too. He's said that he's the establishment's worst nightmare. He says he's too rich too be bought, too independent to care about what his enemies say, too powerful to be stopped. He'll stand up for the American people by standing against the powers-that-be.

Then he turns around and says he'll make deals. "I think the [establishment is] warming up," Trump said this week. "I want to be honest, I have received so many phone calls from people that you would call establishment, from people -- generally speaking ... conservatives, Republicans -- that want to come onto our team. We are getting calls from everybody that it's actually amazing. I'm actually surprised."

Why? Because, says Trump, unlike his chief rival, Senator Ted Cruz, R-Texas, he'll make deals. He's a deal-maker! "Guys like Ted Cruz will never make a deal because he's a strident guy," Trump said. "That's what the country's about really, isn't it?"

And Trump will make deals. He isn't lying. He's friendly with everybody on the Democratic side of the aisle. Here's Trump on

House Minority Leader Nancy Pelosi, D-Calif.: "I think I'm going to be able to get along with Pelosi -- I've always had a good relationship with Nancy Pelosi." Here's Trump on Senate Minority Leader Harry Reid, D-Nev.: He "always treated me nicely. We need that in Washington." Here's Trump on Senator Chuck Schumer, D-N.Y., godfather of amnesty: "I think I'll be able to get along well with Schumer, Chuck Schumer. I was always very good with Schumer. I was close to Schumer in many ways."

For that matter, here's Trump on Hillary Clinton circa 2012: "Hillary Clinton I think is a terrific woman." Here's Trump on President Obama circa 2009: "I think he's doing a really good job. ... He's really a champion."

It's not that Trump represents the establishment. He's still anti-establishment because he's not taking cues from them. He's running his own campaign, and he's following his own advice. But just because you oppose the establishment doesn't mean that you're a conservative. Trump opposes the establishment because he thinks of himself as a political outsider. The base opposes the establishment because they don't want Republicans in the establishment cutting bad deals with Democrats. Which means that Trump's anti-establishment viewpoint doesn't match up with that of the conservative base.

Trump may change Washington, D.C., but not in a way conservatives will like. He could be a Republican Barack Obama, but he won't be a conservative one. And another egomaniac without Constitutional strictures is the last thing we need.

The Establishment Is Dead

February 3, 2016

In Monday's Iowa caucus, Senator Ted Cruz, R-Texas, the man most hated by the Republican establishment, came from behind to nab front-runner Donald Trump. Senator Marco Rubio, R-Fla., the supposed establishment favorite, came in just a point behind Trump. According to conventional wisdom, this should set up a battle royal among anti-establishment Cruz, anti-establishment Trump and establishment Rubio. If Rubio emerges victorious, the pundits explain, the establishment will have lived to fight another day, and put those rowdy conservative grass-roots anti-establishment types in their place.

This is nonsense.

Cruz is the most conservative person in the Republican race. Trump, up until he became the establishment's baton against Cruz, was a thorn in the side of the establishment. And the new establishment darling, Rubio, is arguably the second-most conservative person in the Republican race (the only other contender is Senator Rand Paul). There's a reason the establishment backed then-Republican Florida Governor Charlie Crist over Rubio in 2010.

In fact, there's only one reason the establishment can tolerate Rubio, who is ardently anti-abortion, thoroughly hawkish, and consistently pro-free markets (outside of his bizarre support for sugar subsidies). They support Rubio because he backed the Gang of Eight amnesty bill in 2013. Rubio has been soft on immigration since his days in the Florida state legislature. He briefly adopted Mitt Romney's self-deportation platform in 2012 before flipping left in 2013; then, after serious blowback, he abandoned that position. That's obviously problematic, and a reason for conservatives to question his credentials on that issue. But leaving amnesty aside, calling Rubio "establishment" does a true disservice to the conservative grassroots who elected him in the first place.

So, what does that mean? It means that in the Iowa caucus, openly anti-establishment candidates -- from Trump to Cruz to Rubio to Ben Carson to Rand Paul -- received 88.9 percent of the vote. Jeb Bush, the original establishment favorite, received just 2.8 percent of the vote. John Kasich clocked in at 1.9 percent. Chris Christie received just 1.8 percent.

The story is no different in New Hampshire. There, establishment candidates amount to just 27.6 percent of the electorate, according to the latest RealClearPolitics polling averages. All the talk of the tea party's death was greatly exaggerated -- the tea party took over the Republican Party. The establishment's newfound enthusiasm for Rubio represents a desperation play, an attempt to latch onto the least worst option they can find. But that doesn't mean that Rubio is establishment.

So, conservatives should cheer the results of the Iowa caucus, regardless of which candidate they supported. That doesn't mean the establishment can't rise from the grave - they co-opted tea partyer Rubio once, and may be able to do so again. But it does mean that for the moment, default successful national Republicanism is conservative. And that's a big win for the grassroots.

How Attitude Trumped
Conservative Thought

February 10, 2016

On Monday, grassroots Republican favorite Donald Trump repeated the phrase when an audience member called Ted Cruz a "p----." He came to this conclusion after determining that Cruz wasn't sufficiently gung-ho about waterboarding possible terrorists. Asked to define conservatism at the last Republican debate, Trump stated, "I think it's a person who doesn't want to take overly risks. I think that's a good thing."

On Tuesday, establishment Republican favorite columnist David Brooks of The New York Times wrote a column called "I Miss Barack Obama." In it, he pilloried Senators Marco Rubio, R-Fla., and Ted Cruz, R-Texas, and lamented that Obama "radiates an ethos of integrity, humanity, good manners and elegance that I'm beginning to miss." In October, Brooks defined conservatism thusly: "conservatism stands for intellectual humility, a belief in steady, incremental change, a preference for reform rather than revolution, a respect for hierarchy, precedence, balance and order, and a tone of voice that is prudent, measured and responsible."

Neither of these definitions are correct, of course. But the fact that Trump and Brooks largely agree on the definition of conservatism while fighting each other tooth and nail demonstrates why conservatism is losing.

Both Trump and Brooks think that conservatism is mainly an attitude. It's not a set of principles and policies; it's not a philosophy of human freedom and small government. Instead, conservatism is merely an orientation toward change: Trump wants slow change, and so does Brooks.

So where do they disagree? They disagree about whether conservatism is militant attitude in pursuit of slow change (Trump) or whether conservatism is elegance in pursuit of slow change (Brooks). Trump thinks Brooks is a "p----," presumably; Brooks thinks Trump is a vulgarian.

Neither one is actually conservative, and yet they're fighting for the mantle of conservative leadership.

The problem, of course, is that conservatism has very little to do with attitude. Conservatism demands Constitutionalism, and in the aftermath of a century of progressive growth of government -- including growth at the hands of so-called conservatives -- change need not be gradual. The attitude matters less than the goal. We can have hard-charging conservatives like Mark Levin; we can have 10-dollar-word conservatives like many of the writers at National Review. What we can't have is nonconservatives redefining conservatism as an attitude, and then ignoring the underlying philosophy.

Yet that's precisely what we have in this race. The entire Republican race thus far has avoided policy differentiations in favor of critiques of attitudes. Who is more palatable, the shifty-seeming Cruz, or the smooth-talking Rubio? Who is more worthwhile, the brusque Chris Christie or the milquetoast Jeb Bush?

Who cares?

Republicans have spent so long in the wilderness that they've forgotten what animated them in the first place. At some point, Republicans forgot that their job was to determine the best face for a conservative philosophy, and instead substituted the face for the philosophy. The conservatism simply fell away.

In the battle between David Brooks' pseudoconservatism and Donald Trump's pseudoconservatism, there are no winners, but there is one major loser: conservatism itself. Conservatives need to worry less about how they fight -- whether they wear creased pants or hurl nasty insults -- and instead contemplate why they're fighting in the first place.

The Day the Constitution Died

February 17, 2016

On Saturday, Supreme Court Justice Antonin Scalia, the foremost thinker of the originalist and textualist judicial philosophy, died. It threw constitutional loyalists across the nation into mourning -- not just because Scalia was a brilliant expositor of the founding document, a great defender of the constitutional order, but also because with Scalia's death, Democrats are just one vote on the Court from destroying the Constitution wholesale.

Scalia believed that the Constitution ought to be applied as it was written -- it wasn't poetry, to be interpreted by the self-proclaimed moral superiors of the Supreme Court, but a legal document requiring specific legal interpretation. As Scalia said, "The Constitution says what it says, and it doesn't say anything more. ... Under the guise of interpreting the Constitution and under the banner of a living Constitution, judges, especially those on the Supreme Court, now wield an enormous amount of political power, because they don't just apply the rules that have been written, they create new rules."

With Scalia gone, the left will look to create a vast bevy of new rules designed to destroy constitutional freedoms. Scalia represented the fifth vote on gun rights, freedom of speech and freedom of religion; now, expect the Supreme Court to reinterpret the Second Amendment to allow full-scale gun confiscation, reinterpret freedom of speech to allow "hate speech" legislation and crackdowns on corporate political speech and reinterpret freedom of religion to allow a full-scale government cram down of anti-religious policy on religious individuals and institutions.

Even as conservatives lamented Scalia's death, Republicans held a debate on Saturday night. At that debate, Republican front-runner

Donald Trump demonstrated that even among the Republican electorate, a significant percentage of Americans no longer care about Scalia-like Constitutional separation of powers. Trump is a bloviating loudmouth, a bullying spoiled rich kid who has never been told no. And he aims to govern like one. Put aside Trump's channeling of Michael Moore this week (he said that George W. Bush was responsible for 9/11 and lied to get America into the Iraq War). What's truly important is Trump's vision of governance.

For Trump, everything in life is about Trump. He says he likes Russian dictator Vladimir Putin because Putin "called me a genius, I like him so far, I have to tell you." He says he'll fix the economy personally: "I'm going to save Social Security. I'm going to bring jobs back from China. I'm going to bring back jobs from Mexico and from Japan ... Vietnam, that's the new one. ... I'm the only one who is going to save Social Security, believe me." Everything boils down to Trump fixing the world through the power of his persona.

None of which has any relationship to the Constitution. Scalia's death represents one threat to the future of checks and balances and limited government; Trump's rise as the leading candidate for a party that used to avoid strongmen in favor of those principles represents another type of threat. Both are potentially fatal to the future of the American idea.

When Manliness Goes Missing

February 24, 2016

By most available information, Donald Trump will win the Republican nomination. He's not a conservative in any meaningful sense -- he shifts his positions at whim, preaches about the worth of big government and suggests that he will personally "win for America." But after eight years of Barack Obama's passive-aggressive emasculation of Americans, many conservatives have embraced Trump because of his unbridled masculinity. He's Joe Pesci in "Goodfellas": a toxic dude who's fun to watch, but who might occasionally shoot somebody just for the hell of it. On Fifth Avenue, apparently. And receive plaudits from his followers.

This is the natural effect of the unmanning of American politics.

Obama told Americans for years on end that they were racist, sexist, bigoted homophobes who just didn't understand that our brash, confident attitude alienated people all around the world and led to terrorism against us. Hillary Clinton is running for president on the basis of her X chromosomes; America, she says, needs a female president. Bernie Sanders says that our unchecked aggressive instincts have ill-served us; we need a kinder, gentler America.

Meanwhile, the Republicans have self-castrated. Senator Mitch McConnell, R-Ky., spent years telling conservatives that Obama couldn't be stopped, and that attempts to stop him would be uncivil and counterproductive. Former Speaker of the House John Boehner did the same. So, too, has new Speaker of the House Paul Ryan. George W. Bush ran on the basis of "compassionate" conservatism, implying that traditional conservatism was too musky for metrosexual America. Marco Rubio's brand of politics relies on a feelings-first approach; Rubio said last week, "If a significant percentage of the American family believes that they are being treated differently than everyone else, we have a problem. And we have to address it as a society and as a country." This is pure Obama, Republican-style.

Trump, however, doesn't bother with the niceties. He's a big, swinging set of political testicles. He says, just like a good mafia boss would, that he'll take care of all of your problems. He threatens his political opponents -- he tells protesters he wants to see them roughed up, and he tells donors to his opposition that he'll target them. He swears like a sailor in public. He unmans his competition: Jeb! Bush is "low-energy," Ted Cruz a "p----," Ben Carson a "pedophile," Rubio a "lightweight," Carly Fiorina a problem "face." He's gross and chauvinistic: He calls women "pieces of a--" and rips Megyn Kelly for bleeding from her "wherever."

He is, in short, a man in the locker room, in all of his ugly glory. He's toxic masculinity. He's not a gentleman, and he's proud of it. He's here to win, and he'll bully, threaten, and beat you until you submit.

Normally, the masculinity gap in American politics could be filled by an upstanding man -- a man, yes, but one tied to values, a man who uses the aggressive instinct in pursuit of defending the innocent and punishing the guilty. But the feminist movement has made such men obsolete. Men were simply too dangerous; it was safer to emasculate them. Now men are expected to be betas; the only alphas left are toxic alphas willing to break every taboo and violate every standard.

There's still a space for masculinity in American politics. But thanks to the vacuum of decent men, indecent men rise. Men like Donald Trump.

The Leftist Fascists Take Over College Campuses

March 2, 2016

Last Thursday, all hell broke loose at California State University Los Angeles. Hundreds of students gathered to chant slogans, block entrances and exits to the student union auditorium, rough up those who wished to enter, pull the fire alarm, and trap other students inside that auditorium under threat of violence. Police officers stood aside and allowed that mob to violate basic safety protocols, reportedly at the behest of the school administration.

Why?

Because I was coming to speak.

I had been scheduled to speak at Cal State Los Angeles for weeks. Young America's Foundation had organized the Fred R. Allen Lecture Series; CSULA represented the kickoff event. Student activists worked hard to publicize the event. Two separate radical professors at the university objected publicly to it, with one challenging "white supremacist" students to wrestle him, and another asking on Facebook, "I say this event is a problem...What we go'n do y'all?!?!"

Then, the Monday before the big conflagration, the president of the university, William Covino, summarily canceled my speech. "After careful consideration, I have decided that it will be best for our campus community if we reschedule Ben Shapiro's appearance for a later date, so that we can arrange for him to appear as part of a group of speakers with differing viewpoints on diversity. Such an event will better represent our university's dedication to the free exchange of ideas and the value of considering multiple viewpoints," Covino stated in Orwellian fashion.

I told Covino to stick it -- this was viewpoint discrimination, and I would show up anyway.

After days of silence, Covino must have determined that he didn't want to risk the legal consequences of barring me, so just two hours before the event, he backed down, adding, "I strongly disagree with Mr. Shapiro's views."

By the time we reached campus, the near-riot had begun. I had to be ushered through a back door by armed security as well as uniformed police. Helicopters circled the area; news trucks parked along the street. The room in which I was slated to speak was nearly empty, because the student protesters had blocked all the doors and were pushing around anyone who wanted to enter. One reporter was assaulted three times; one of the people who wanted to attend my speech was pushed to the ground and kicked. Police smuggled the students in four at a time through the back door until students blocked that door, too. Halfway through my speech, the fire alarm went off. I spoke through it.

When the speech ended, I asked security if I, along with the other students, could go out to confront the protesters. The campus police told me they couldn't guarantee my safety or that of any of those listening to me if we chose to walk outside. Instead, they'd have to spirit me away through a separate building with a large coterie of armed and uniformed police, stuff me into the back of a van, and then escort me from campus with motorcycles flashing their lights.

This is America in 2016, on a state-funded university campus.

And it shouldn't be surprising.

We have spent two generations turning college campuses from places to learn job skills to places to indoctrinate leftism and inculcate an intolerant view of the world that insists on silencing opposition. We have made campuses a fascist "safe space" on behalf of the left. Anyone who disagrees must be shut down, or threatened or hurt.

It's not just college campuses, either. We've entered an era of politics in which baseless feelings count more than facts, in which political correctness means firing those with different viewpoints, in which government actors insist that they can police negative thoughts. We're on the edge of freedom's end, and many Americans don't even see it.

They would have had they been at CSULA that day. And they will soon enough if they don't stand up for their rights today.

Three Reasons Conservatives Should Fear The Trump Phenomenon

March 9, 2016

Donald Trump's candidacy is scary.

Trump isn't frightening because he's anything special personally. He's just a warmed-over mash-up of Pat Buchanan and Ross Perot, a spoiled brat billionaire eccentric with a history of position flipping and bullying foolishness. He has authoritarian tendencies on a personal level, and no awareness of the Constitution or its importance. In other words, he's Barack Obama if Obama weren't ideologically driven and suddenly experienced a precipitous drop in IQ.

So what's so scary about Trump?

First, the idolatry of a certain segment of his following. Trump has drawn some of the worst elements of American life to his campaign. To be sure, most of his supporters are decent Americans who find his approach to politics a revelation: He's an outsider, someone who will "get things done." Some of his followers identify with his hard-line position on illegal immigration and his dislike of free trade, even though Trump could flip those positions in a heartbeat if he felt the political necessity to do so.

But some of Trump's supporters go beyond that. Some are driven by the pure worship of the strong man. Like Obama's cultish support base, some Trump supporters are willing to follow him anywhere, to justify any misbehavior, to view any opposition to Trump as a sort of irreligious disloyalty. When Trump asked voters to hold up their right arms and pledge their allegiance to him, media mocked him as a Hitlerian figure. He's no Hitler -- he's not nearly as smart, as ideologically consistent, or as dangerous. He's a barroom prince. Instead, we should be concerned with the increasing tendency of Americans, both left and right, to hero-worship politicians to the point of blindness.

Which leads to the second reason Trump should concern conservatives: his appeal to nasty causes. Trump desperately wants popularity. He gauges his success by the size of his crowds, his success in the polls, and the compliments he receives in the press. He'll talk up Russian dictator thug Vladimir Putin so long as Putin calls him "brilliant." And he'll go easy on former KKK leader David Duke if Duke endorses him. Trump's lack of moral principle makes him an easy mark for some of the worst people on the planet. Combine the fact that he is drawn to those who would manipulate him with the fact that he has a worshipful crowd following him, and it's not difficult to see how the Trump movement ends in tragedy.

Finally, conservatives should oppose Trump full-throatedly because he's perverting conservatism. Even as he cultivates idolatry and massages white supremacists and global tyrants, Trump proclaims that he's a conservative. Many of us who have spent a lifetime fighting against the false notion that conservatism is a toxic brew of secret racism and fascism; Trump's rise provides easy fodder for the opposition. And his followers refuse to acknowledge that Trump has little to do with conservatism. Instead, they allow him to use the mantle of Lincoln and Reagan and the founders to shield his own egocentric rise from criticism.

Trump's no conservative -- he's a leftist at heart, a man convinced of his own power, a man willing to abandon all principle to serve himself and his allies. His followers think they're his allies, but that only lasts so long as they follow him. Yes, conservatives should fear Trump's rise. And they should resist it however and wherever possible.

What a Trump Nomination Means for Conservatives

March 16, 2016

For years, conservatives have told themselves the pretty bedtime story that they represent a silent majority in America -- that most Americans want smaller government, individual rights and personal responsibility. We've suggested that if only we nominated precisely the right guy who says the right words -- some illegally grown Ronald Reagan clone, perhaps -- we'd win.

Donald Trump's impending nomination puts all of that to bed.

There can be no doubt: The Republican Party has successful killed the legacy of Ronald Reagan. By consistently moving to the left in every presidential election, by granting the left its general premise that government is generally a tool for good rather than a risky potential instrument of tyranny and by teaching Americans that the problem isn't government itself, but who runs it, Republicans have ensured that the vast majority of Americans no longer hold to conservative principles.

In fact, a significant swath of Republicans themselves don't believe in conservative principles. Trump, obviously, is no conservative. He's a protectionist on trade -- a position that smacks of populist pandering rather than informed conservative economics. He believes in an authoritarian executive branch designed to make deals that achieve a win for Americans, rather than a heavily circumscribed executive branch with prescribed powers of enforcement. He believes that judges sign bills, that legislators exist merely to bargain with the great man in charge and that the military exists to serve as his personal armed forces.

All of this attracts people.

The angrier Trump gets, the more he talks about how he's going to set things right rather than giving Americans the power to do so themselves, and the more Americans flock to him.

So, let's look at the facts. Today, at low ebb, Trump garners approximately 4 in 10 Republican voters. Let's assume that at least half of those Americans aren't conservative -- a fair guess, given that many have admitted bias in polls in favor of government interventionism in the economy, a sneaking love for government entitlement programs and a strong position against immigration -- not for safety reasons, but to prevent economic competition. Meanwhile, more than 4 in 10 Americans support Democrats outright.

This means that at least 6 in 10 Americans support a big government vision of the world.

Which means conservatives have failed.

In order to rebuild, conservatives must recognize that they think individually; leftists think institutionally. While the left took over the universities -- now bastions of pantywaist fascism hell-bent on destroying free speech -- the right slept. While the left took over the public education system wholesale, the right fled to private schools and homeschooling. While the left utilized popular culture as a weapon, conservatives supposedly withdrew and turned off their televisions.

Withdrawal, it turns out, wasn't the best option.

Fighting back on all fronts is. Republicans need to worry less about the next election and significantly more about building a movement of informed Americans who actually understand American values. That movement must start with outreach to parents, and it must extend to the takeover of local institutions or defunding of government institutions outright. The left has bred a generation of Americans who do not recognize the American ideals of the Founding Fathers. Pretending otherwise means flailing uselessly as demagogues like Trump become faux-conservative standard-bearers.

The Day Freedom Died in Cuba

March 23, 2016

In 1959, Fidel Castro and his communist henchmen put a bullet through the head of freedom. Proclaiming the era of equality, they threw dissidents in jail or shot them, cracked down on free speech, closed their markets and seized private property. Thousands of Cubans fled to the liberty of the United States. Over the decades, hundreds of thousands of Cubans left the island any way they could. Learned men floated battered cars 90 miles toward Florida in the hope that they would reach land; young women smuggled their babies into rickety old boats in the desperate desire to escape perennial servitude.

But the spirit of freedom never died. Freedom can never be crushed, after all, so long as freedom lives elsewhere. And for sixty years, it lived just beyond the horizon. President after president signaled support for the aspirations of the Cuban people for something beyond the petty tyranny of the Castros.

Then along came President Obama.

This week, President Obama visited Cuba. There, he was snubbed on the tarmac by tin-pot dictator Raul Castro; he took a staged photo before a massive building-sized mural of genocidal murderer Che Guevara; he smiled and bowed to Castro when they met. Castro treated Obama to a harangue about America's moral inferiority, blustering, "We defend human rights." He adds, "Actually, we find it inconceivable that a government does not defend and ensure the right to health care, any patient, social security, food provision and development, equal pay and the rights of children." Obama nodded along, then stated placidly, "I personally would not disagree with that." He then added, idiotically, "The goal of the human rights dialogue is not for the United States to dictate to Cuba how they should govern themselves, but to make sure that we are having a frank and candid conversation around this issue. And hopefully that we can learn from each other."

The United States does not need to learn from Cuba; Cuba needs to learn from the United States. But in his desire to glorify his own name, in his even deeper desire to level the global economic playing field, and in his *greatest* desire to tear out Americanism at the roots, Obama kowtows to some of the worst people on the planet.

And kowtow he does. After that awkward exchange, Raul Castro grabbed Obama's wrist; Obama went limp, and allowed Castro to raise his hanging hand high in the air. Then, hours later in a press briefing, the State Department did not directly say anything about the crackdown on hundreds of dissidents who were jailed just before his arrival. The Cubans arrested one of the dissidents' leaders scheduled to meet with Obama. Ben Rhodes, Obama's national security advisor, shrugged all of that off, stating that the United States understands that the Cuban government sees these political prisoners as criminals under Cuban law. Obama himself did not directly say whether he would give Castro a list of political prisoners for release.

In other words, Obama went to Cuba with the express purpose of snuffing out the last hope that Americans would be willing to stand with freedom. In the end, he won't succeed. America remains free, and Obama's self-congratulatory virtue signaling on behalf of a terroristic authoritarian nightmare doesn't change that. But Obama's actions in legitimizing one of the worst regimes in modern history will damn at least one more generation to their tender mercies.

How the Clintons Made Donald Trump

March 30, 2016

Donald Trump is a boor. He's a vulgarian, a liar, an ignoramus. He has only the most cursory grasp of policy, a stentorian voice and a great big set of self-assurance. He's winning the Republican nomination.

Why?

It is partly because of the Clintons.

While the media point and laugh at the Trump reality show carnival, they forget that the Clintons originally took us all to the circus. This week, we found out that Hillary Clinton's email scandal now occupies the attention of 147 FBI agents, and that she will be questioned by the FBI. We found out that her pig husband allegedly snorted cocaine off the table of one of his former lovers in 1983, as well as gallivanted around her place wearing her nightie while playing the saxophone. And the indispensable Judicial Watch released information that the Obama administration is withholding draft indictments of Hillary Clinton, including an indictment over the Whitewater case during her husband's first term in office.

Nobody bat an eye.

This is the world to which Americans have become accustomed. We've been immunized to scandal. It's difficult to come up with a scandal that could damage Trump. Caught in bed with two hookers? That's just because he's got such lovely hands. Caught beating a dog with a tire iron? The man has passion. Trump is the apex of black socks politics. As the old children's rhyme goes: "Black socks, they never get dirty,/ the longer you wear them, the blacker they get."

We all embraced black socks politics thanks to the Clintons.

The Clintons dragged the office of the presidency through the muck. Now, they're trying to rehabilitate themselves at the expense of Trump. It won't work. Trump doesn't even pretend to have standards: He cheated on his first wife with his second, his second with his third, and presumably at some point will cheat on his third with his fourth (should he live so long). But nobody cares.

Meanwhile, the National Enquirer runs a sourceless, evidenceless story about Senator Ted Cruz, R-TX, supposedly shtupping a series of women not his wife, and the media go ballistic. That's because it's significantly more dangerous in this political day and age to have standards than to abandon all standards before you get started. Bill Clinton can get away with being human because nobody expects anything else. But so can Hillary Clinton, and so can Trump. Those who aspire to something higher have farther to fall.

And so, we're going to be increasingly treated to a series of candidates from both sides of the aisle with checkered pasts and no principles. After all, principles tie you down, force you to behave and put you in the awkward position of having to act decently. Better to skip the standards and go straight for the scandal. If you have enough of them early on and often enough, your candidacy becomes downright unkillable, like an antibiotic-resistant virus.

Hence Trump. Hence Clinton. Hence prospective presidential candidates Kanye West, Kim Kardashian and Jenna Jameson. Why not? After all, at least they're not hypocrites. They're exactly who they say they are. No scandal can touch them.

Trump Whines and Whines
Until He Loses

April 6, 2016

On Tuesday night, Senator Ted Cruz, R-TX, won a sweeping victory over 2016 Republican presidential front-runner Donald Trump in Wisconsin. Cruz won virtually every demographic, nearly 50 percent of the vote and the vast bulk of the delegates. It's becoming increasingly clear that Trump could fail to reach the necessary 1,237 delegates in order to win the nomination outright on the first ballot at the convention. If so, there's no way he wins the nomination at all.

That's because Trump has made himself radioactive.

If Trump had disappeared from the American political scene after his big win in Arizona, he'd have wrapped up the nomination by now. Instead, he defended his lying campaign manager, Corey Lewandowski, after Lewandowski was charged with battery for allegedly grabbing, yanking and bruising a reporter; tweeted nastily about Heidi Cruz's looks; repeatedly suggested that Cruz had violated federal law without evidence; trotted out surrogates to slander anti-Trump women as Cruz's adulteresses; flipped his abortion position four times in less than three days; found himself on the short end of the interview stick with a Wisconsin radio host; labeled health care, housing and education as key functions of the federal government; accused the Republican National Committee and state delegations of attempting to "steal" the nomination from him by engaging in traditional delegate politics; and stated that he would likely select Supreme Court justices who would investigate Hillary Clinton's email server, for starters.

The more Trump talks, the worse he sounds.

Now, Trump's supporters keep saying he's just learning the ropes. After all, he's never run for political office before, so a few hiccups are to be expected. But Trump continues to demonstrate a complete inability to learn. After losing Wisconsin, did Trump turn down his "Spinal Tap" speakers from volume 11 to 8? Of course not. He turned the volume up to 12 with a campaign statement that bragged that Trump's 13-point blowout at Cruz's hands was actually a big win in which he "withstood the onslaught of the establishment yet again." The statement also stated openly, and without evidence, that Cruz had illegally coordinated with his super PACs, and slammed Cruz as being "worse than a puppet -- he is a Trojan horse, being used by the party bosses attempting to steal the nomination from Mr. Trump."

Trump's campaign is flailing because it's not a campaign; it's a self-produced vanity reality TV special. Trump didn't bother to learn the delegate rules because he couldn't be bothered to do so. He doesn't bother to learn the ins and outs of his own policies because, hey, why bother when people flock to you for shouting slogans about building walls? Last month, he fired his data team manager and elevated the second in command. But the second in command apparently doesn't know politics, or even how to access the data itself.

But don't worry: Trump has a very good brain and hires all the best people.

By the time of the Republican National Convention, Trump will be 70-years-old. Sadly, he has significantly less self-control than my 2-year-old daughter. He's spent his entire life being handed things: money, fame, female companionship. Now he can't understand why he's not being handed the nomination. So, like Veruca Salt in "Willy Wonka and the Chocolate Factory," he'll scream.

It won't work. Trump joked months ago that his strategy was to "keep whining and whining until I win." But now he's beginning to lose. And the whining won't stop anytime soon.

The Suicidal Left Throws
Bill Clinton Over

April 13, 2016

This week, the Bernie Sanders revolution finally ate its own. The vultures of the hard left forced former Secretary of State Hillary Clinton to sink her own carnivorous beak into the withered flesh of her titular husband, former President Bill Clinton, denouncing his key legislative achievements and relegating him to the dustbin of history.

The hubbub began after Bill Clinton ran into opposition from Black Lives Matter activists at one of his speeches. He proceeded to shred them -- accurately -- for their inane focus on supposed police brutality and criminal justice bias rather than saving actual black lives: "I don't know how you would characterize the gang leaders who got 13-year-old kids hopped up on crack and sent them out onto the streets to murder other African-American children. Maybe you thought they were good citizens. ... You are defending the people who killed the lives you say matter. Tell the truth. You are defending the people who cause young people to go out and take guns. ... They say the welfare reform bill increased poverty. Then why did we have the largest drop in African-American poverty in history when I was president?"

All of this is true.

But for the left, truth must be discarded in favor of the narrative. And so, Clinton was raked over the coals for gainsaying the mythology of the left: that the criminal justice system penalizes innocent young black men disproportionately, that their sentences are longer than whites', and that police enforcement disproportionately targets young black men.

And Hillary Clinton, in order to stave off the onslaught of a 7,000-year-old socialist loonbag, bravely threw Bill onto a political grenade. "I have been consistently speaking out about what I would do as president," she said after Bill's implosion, "And I think it's important for people to recognize we have work to do, that there were a lot of people very scared and concerned about high crime back in the day. And now we've got to say, OK, we have to deal with the consequences. And one of the consequences is, in my view, (the) overincarceration of people who should not have been in the criminal justice system."

Never mind that Bill's decision to fight criminality resulted, at least in part, in the single greatest prolonged reduction in crime in American history. What's important is that Hillary wants to win the nomination. It doesn't matter how many young black people have to die in order for slightly older black people to vote for her.

And die they will. The murder rate is up dramatically over the past two years in cities ranging from Baltimore to New Orleans, from St. Louis to Chicago to New York. This is what happens when the mythology of police as villains destroys their capacity to act as heroes. The high crime neighborhoods are left to those who commit crime.

But Hillary Clinton doesn't care. Neither does Bernie. All that matters is continuing Democratic victory at the expense of truth and American lives.

Your Daughter Must Pee Next to a Man, and You Will Be Compelled to Agree

April 20, 2016

The rules of bigotry according to the left represent a constantly shifting kaleidoscope of nonsense. This week, we learned that if you don't want your small daughter peeing next to a giant man who thinks he is a woman, you are a bigot; if you are a woman who is uncomfortable with a man who thinks he is a woman whipping out his male genitalia to urinate in front of you, you are a bigot; if you are a religious person who doesn't want to participate in an activity you consider sinful, you are a bigot.

Conversely, if you are a man who thinks he is a woman and you want to force a small girl to pee next to you, you are a freedom fighter; if you are a large man who thinks he is a woman and you want to be one of the girls, right down to hulking into a Macy's ladies room, you are a hero; if you are a gay man and you want to force a religious person to serve you, you are a hero.

If all of this seems odd, that's because it is.

It's obviously logically incoherent, to begin with. The left insists that a man who believes he is a woman must be treated as one, even if his biology dictates that he is a male. However, if a man believes he is a man, he cannot discuss vital issues of national import (like abortion) since he lacks the vital prerequisite: a womb. Men cannot understand women, the logic seems to run, unless they *are* women. But men cannot be women, of course, except in the fevered imaginations of people on the left. Even the left doesn't believe that: Leftists simultaneously want to enshrine unchangeable sexual differences (although, according to them, men and women are inherently and unchangingly different with regard to their abortion perspectives) and deny that these differences exist in the first place. (Caitlyn Jenner's twig and berries are irrelevant to the issue of gender, they say).

"This is nonsense," you say.

"Shut up," they say.

In the end, leftists don't have to be coherent -- they just have to control the government gun.

The baseline definition of freedom in Western Civilization has been this: You do not get to force me to serve you, and you do not get to force me to think the way you want me to think. As follows, you cannot force me to think that you are a woman if you are a biological man. You cannot force me to spend my taxpayer dollars to pretend along with your mental illness. You cannot force me to run my business as you see fit because I have no affirmative duty to you.

But the left doesn't believe in freedom -- except the freedom to destroy the right. Thus, leftists believe that Bruce Springsteen has an absolute right to cancel concerts in North Carolina, but that bakers in North Carolina can't stop baking wedding cakes for same-sex couples. The left believes that the government *must* compel elevated pay rates for women, but government should compel men to be treated as women based on their subjective feelings on the subject.

The kaleidoscope of leftist morality never stops shifting. But in the end, only one moral counts: the left's ultimate insistence on use of government force to compel obedience to their kaleidoscopic morality.

What Is Democratic?

April 27, 2016

Having devoured the meanings of the words "establishment" and "conservative" with some fava beans and a nice chianti, Donald Trump has spent the last several weeks cannibalizing yet another word that used to have meaning: democratic. Trump says that the delegate system is undemocratic; he says that caucuses that do not swing his way are undemocratic; he says that candidates cutting deals with one another to stay in or out of particular states is undemocratic; he says that if he does not win the Republican nomination while carrying a plurality of votes, that's undemocratic, too.

All of this assumes, of course, that Trump is the embodiment of the will of the people. By no other definition of "democratic" are any of his accusations remotely true.

First off, there is nothing undemocratic about delegates. Delegates are merely representatives. Some delegates are chosen by popular vote and are bound to vote in favor of the candidate selected at the primary election; some are not. There's nothing wrong with either system. Arguing against bound delegates is arguing against referenda; arguing against unbound delegates is arguing against basic republicanism.

Second, caucuses *are* democratic. People meet democratically and select delegates to represent them at the caucus. These delegates are selected, presumably, based on the trust of those who vote for them. Trump had no complaints about the caucus system in Nevada. He only hated the system in Colorado, where he lost.

Third, candidates cutting deals with one another other isn't undemocratic, unless it's also undemocratic for Trump to call for candidates to drop out of the race based on lack of success. In either case, candidates make their own decisions about whether to put themselves forward for election. The notion that it is undemocratic for Ohio Governor John Kasich to abandon the Indiana caucus in order to let Texas Senator Ted Cruz stop Trump there, is just as silly as the argument that it is undemocratic for Republicans to refuse President Obama's court nominees an up-or-down vote.

Fourth, plurality does not equal majority. The point of the delegate process is to generate an artificial majority from a plurality. That's what happened in 2008, when Senator John McCain, R-AZ won just 46 percent of the popular vote, but a significant majority of delegates. If Trump can't pull off that feat, that's his own fault. Most Republicans don't want Trump. Most Republicans don't want Cruz or Kasich, either. That inability to choose means that delegates that Republican voters selected will now perform what is, in essence, a run-off election with the remaining candidates.

If we could remake all the rules right now from scratch, I'd propose a system of proportional representation in all primaries: Compress the schedule so it doesn't take months to run through the process. If nobody hits a majority, cut off the bottom candidates, then re-run the election process again. That's just my idea, though -- and there's no reason that my idea ought to trump the ideas of the grass-roots activists of various states.

Trump's redefinition of "undemocratic" is merely ad hoc politicking, as always. No substantive changes would have satisfied Trump. And when it comes to the definition of "undemocratic," threatening riots in Cleveland if you don't get your way tops the list.

The Left's Thought-Fascism Hits ESPN

May 4, 2016

For baseball fans, the performance of Boston Red Sox pitcher Curt Schilling in the 2004 American League Championships ranks among the most memorable gutsy plotlines of all time.

The Red Sox, fighting a World Series winless streak dating back to 1918, were down three games to none to their archrival, the New York Yankees. The Sox then won two straight games. In the crucial Game Six, Schilling was slated to start, despite a torn tendon sheath in his right ankle that required medical staff to literally suture his tendon to deeper tissue. He proceeded to throw seven innings, giving up just one run, and giving us the immoral image of blood seeping through his sock as he dragged his team to victory.

ESPN created a "30 for 30" documentary on the series titled "Four Days In October." The original documentary ran one hour and five minutes, and included a 17-minute segment focusing on Schilling's heroics.

When ESPN re-aired the documentary this week, however, the 17-minute Schilling segment was simply cut.

Why?

Two weeks ago, Schilling posted on Facebook that men who believe they're women shouldn't use the women's bathroom. He shared a meme with a rather hideous gentleman in a skirt, and a leather top with cutouts for his man boobs and stomach, wearing a blonde wig. The caption: "LET HIM IN! To the restroom with your daughter or else you're a narrow minded, judgmental, unloving, racist bigot who needs to die!" Schilling added: "A man is a man no matter what they call themselves. I don't care what they are, who they sleep with, men's room was designed for the penis, women's not so much. Now you need laws telling us differently? Pathetic."

This logic is, of course, inarguable. But it led ESPN to fire him nonetheless, stating: "ESPN is an inclusive company. Curt Schilling has been advised that his conduct was unacceptable and his employment with ESPN has been terminated."

By inclusive, ESPN does not mean ideologically inclusive. They simply mean that if you do not kowtow to politically correct idiocies about men magically becoming women, you will not be tolerated. ESPN is the same channel that rewarded Caitlyn Jenner, nee Bruce, the Arthur Ashe Courage Award for getting a misguided boob job, facial reconstruction surgeries and hormone treatments that will not solve his underlying mental illness. Pointing out that Caitlyn is still a man, however, will get you fired from that same network.

Not only that, but you will be memory-holed. Any person can be wiped from history with a Hillary Clinton-esque cloth at any time if he or she violates the prevailing leftist orthodoxy. Mike Tyson can still star in multiple "30 for 30" episodes after being convicted of rape. But Schilling must be excised from one of the most crucial sporting series in baseball history because he thinks men with penises are still men.

Every area of American life has now been transformed into an enforcement mechanism for leftist groupthink. Entertainment. Education. Even sports.

Conservatives spend all their time and energy focusing on elections. But the real battles are fought in the cultural space, on supposedly minor issues like the employment of All-Star and borderline-hall-of-famer Curt Schilling. If conservatives fail to realize that, elections are only the beginning of their losing streak.

5 Lessons Trump's Nomination Should Teach Republicans

May 10, 2016

We all got it wrong.

Everybody who wrote Donald Trump off as a political charlatan destined to flame out; everybody who called Trump a clown who would return to his reality show and leave us all alone; everybody who suggested that this circus couldn't -- couldn't! -- continue...we were all wrong. Perhaps we were guilty of believing that Trump's mistakes would break out into the mainstream rather than dying slow deaths on cable television. Perhaps we thought that voters would wake up to Trump's bombastic narcissism and turn away. Perhaps, as statistician Nate Silver put it, we were guilty of not predicting "that the Republican Party would lose its f---ing mind."

Whatever the rationale, Trump is surely a shock to everyone but political commentator Ann Coulter and a few other Trump stalwarts.

Now it's time to take away a few lessons.

First, failure to utilize ideological purity tests leads to the rise of leftist candidates within your own party. The bizarre paradox of Trumpian thinking is that the same people complaining about Republicans caving to President Obama want to nominate a lifelong left-leaning ad hoc politician with no centralizing principle other than his own glorification, a man who brags openly that he will cut deals with Democrats. When conservatives object, these Trump fans point to the GOP nominations of former Gov. Mitt Romney, creator of Obamacare, and Sen. John McCain, creator of campaign finance reform and amnesty. They're being hypocritical. McCain and Romney were, by any measure, more conservative overall than Trump. But the feeling that conservatism doesn't matter any longer is hard to quell when, to so many major Republicans, it simply didn't matter that much in 2008 and 2012.

Second, ignoring social issues means that the only way to appeal to disgruntled blue-collar voters is by moving left on economics. There's been a good deal of loose talk about Trump's appeal with disenchanted white voters who didn't show up for Romney. And Trump does indeed appeal to them with lies about the efficacy of tariffs and taxing the rich, which is straight from the Bernie Sanders playbook. These people used to vote Republican -- before the Republican Party decided to toss social policy out the window to pander to New Yorkers like Trump.

Third, moral narrative is far more important than policy knowledge. Trump knows less about policy than my 4-day-old child, and cares less about the Constitution than my boy. But that doesn't matter because he's fighting the "establishment," by which Trump means everyone who disagrees with him. Because he's conflating his "establishment" with a political establishment that insists on cutting deals with President Obama, Republican voters bought in.

Fourth, when there are no good guys, character doesn't matter. One Indiana voter was asked last week about the fact that Trump lies constantly. She said that all politicians lie, and that at least Trump lies differently than other politicians. That's odd logic, but it's true: When all politicians are automatically deemed liars, Trump's lack of character and credibility fades into the woodwork.

Fifth, lack of institutional trust leads to the rise of protofascists, not to a general allegiance to liberty. We hate the media, but instead of seeking honest members of the media, we revel in people who lie to the media and get away with it -- people like Trump. We hate the corrupt political establishment, but instead of seeking people who will abide by Constitutional limitations and minimize the role of government in our lives, we seek a strong man, a *bad* strong man, to break apart the system.

Trump's rise both reflects and foreshadows an ugly future for the country. I hope I'm as wrong on that prediction as I was about Trump's rise.

The Media Have Destroyed
Hillary Clinton

May 18, 2016

On Tuesday, The Hill ran a piece with the hilarious title "Hillary's unlikely ally: The media." The media, of course, have been in Hillary Clinton's camp since the start. The vast majority of media figures are Democrats, and one of them, ABC News' George Stephanopoulos, has written openly of his love for his former boss.

But here's the irony: The media have destroyed Clinton.

They've destroyed her unintentionally, of course. They did so by shielding her from the sort of character attacks Donald Trump has weathered for decades; they did so by pulling the plug on guests who mentioned her husband's history of sexual peccadillos and sexual-assault allegations; they did so by dismissing any critiques of her handling of the Benghazi mess as "sexist"; they did so by talking up Clinton as the inevitable First Female President.

The media had no choice but to do this because Clinton is a terrible candidate. She's off-putting and unlikeable, programmatic and lacking improvisational ability. To protect the ruler, the Roman Praetorian Guard had to form a phalanx. The media did so for Clinton for decades.

All of this left her vulnerable.

As a candidate, Clinton is like the Bubble Boy: She's been placed inside the warm cocoon of an all-embracing leftist establishment, never exposed to the normal viruses of everyday politics. The minute she exits that protective bubble, she's hit with those viruses -- and she has no immune system to help her fight them.

Take, for example, Trump's latest line of attack on Clinton. She trotted out the usual "war on women" routine to attack Trump. His response: "Amazing that Crooked Hillary can do a hit ad on me concerning women when her husband was the WORST abuser of woman in U.S. political history." This is both accurate and on point. In the past, those who have repeated the same talking point on CNN have been cut off, a la Kurt Schlichter. But Trump has around 8.26 million Twitter followers and an unending torrent of media coverage, so Clinton will now have to answer. And her usual answer -- talking down to Americans and tut-tutting away accusations -- won't cut it. Not when she has an attack dog like Trump on her tail.

How about Trump? Trump has been made almost impervious to scandal thanks to media attention. The media have treated Trump as a plane-hopping playboy for years -- a cad and a rogue, a charming billionaire "winner." Trump is like black socks: He never gets dirty, and the longer you wear him, the blacker he gets. It's impossible to identify dirt on a man plastered with mud.

Clinton, by contrast, has been portrayed as pure. She has remained untouched, except by the clutching claws of grimy Republican reptiles. What happens when Trump bulls right through the media ropes and takes the attack directly to Clinton's character?

Nothing good will come for Clinton.

The media subsidized Clinton into a position of power. She's now so vulnerable that a 74-year-old charisma-free socialist nearly took her down. Now she's got a worse virus: a case of the Trumps. Her immune system has been so compromised that she may be politically terminal.

Is Hillary Clinton the Only Innocent Person in a 10-Mile Radius?

May 25, 2016

Hillary Clinton is as pure as the driven snow, at least according to Hillary Clinton.

Clinton will tell you how honest and transparent she is, right after cackling hysterically to stall for time. She will tell you that she always cooperates with law enforcement, that she has attempted to turn over all materials to relevant authorities, that it's just one giant coincidence her friends and family are constantly being swept up in prosecutorial dragnets.

It isn't a coincidence.

Just look at the people with whom Clinton surrounds herself.

Her husband, former President Bill Clinton, is a serial philanderer, a perjurer, a sexual assailant and an accused rapist.

Clinton's former Chief of Staff Cheryl Mills stalked out of an FBI interview after being asked about Clinton's emails. Mills worked as a close assistant to Clinton back during the go-go 1990s. According to Judicial Watch, she helped prevent the Clintons from turning over 1.8 million emails to that organization during litigation. Mills was also placed in charge of document production for the State Department on the Benghazi investigation. According to Gregory Hicks, the second-ranking U.S. diplomat in Libya at the time of the attack, lawyers told him not to talk to Congress.

Clinton's assistant, Huma Abedin, has been dragged into the Clinton email-server scandal. Even after she left Clinton's staff at the State Department, Clinton granted her "special government employee" status even as she took pay from the Clinton Foundation.

Abedin's husband is, of course, former Congressman Anthony "Carlos Danger" Weiner.

Clinton's chief fundraiser for years was former Virginia Governor Terry McAuliffe. He's now under investigation by the FBI and the Department of Justice for fundraising improprieties, including his time at the Clinton Global Initiative. He personally guaranteed the Clintons' loan for their Chappaqua home.

Clinton's foreign-policy guru is Bill Clinton's former aide Sidney Blumenthal, a radical-leftist hatchet man so corrupt that the Obama administration refused to allow Clinton to hire him during her role as secretary of state. Nonetheless, the Clinton Foundation paid him $10,000 per month, even as he sent her memos about foreign policy that included subjects upon which he was doing separate business.

So, is Clinton's association with a number of suspicious characters just a giant coincidence? Or, perhaps, is it a sign that Clinton herself is corrupt and surrounds herself with other corrupt individuals willing to protect her?

It's hard to believe the former, given that Clinton sticks by her corrupt friends for decades. Corruption surrounds her like the cloud of dust that always seems to follow Pig-Pen. That won't change if she's placed in the White House -- it will get worse. Power always makes corruption worse. Clinton should know: She's the only first lady ever fingerprinted by the FBI, and she'll presumably be the first secretary of state interviewed by the FBI. As president, she'd make her husband's deeply corrupt administration pale in comparison.

So no, Clinton can't be trusted. There's a reason polls show that even fewer Americans trust her than the narcissistic pathological liar Donald Trump. All of which means that this election cycle now pits the two most dishonest people in the history of American electoral politics against each other.

Notes From a Neo-Nazi Cuckservative

June 1, 2016

Last week, California State University, Los Angeles held a "healing space" event to provide a safe forum for students and professors to unleash their feelings about my campus speech in February, sponsored by the Young America's Foundation. That speech, you may recall, was originally canceled by university President William Covino. After I decided to go to the campus anyway, hundreds of screaming students blocked doorways, assaulted prospective speechgoers and pulled the fire alarm mid-speech. Professors egged on the protesters; one even threatened student organizers. I was forced to enter through a back door and exit surrounded by a full phalanx of armed and uniformed officers, thanks to the near-riotous conditions outside.

So, naturally, the professors and students who caused the commotion had some hurt feelings.

At their little get-together, Covino announced he "would have never invited anybody like Ben Shapiro" to campus. Covino fretted that "very tragically and unfortunately," somebody like me could show up on campus again. Meanwhile, Professor Melina Abdullah, chair of the university's Pan-African Studies department, said that I had advocated "anti-blackness," and then called me a "neo-Nazi." After realizing that it would be odd to label an Orthodox Jew a "neo-Nazi," she shifted her language slightly, saying, "A neo-KKK member -- let's call him that." She said that students came to her feeling "traumatized" by a speech they probably never heard, feeling "brutalized, physically, emotionally and mentally."

I spent the bulk of my speech talking about how racial diversity was irrelevant -- diversity of viewpoint mattered. This was enough to drive chaos and insanity at the school for months. Apparently, quoting Dr. Martin Luther King Jr. -- which I did during the speech -- makes me a "neo-KKK member."

Meanwhile, David Duke, former Ku Klux Klan grand wizard, has labeled me an enemy of the KKK. I've been hit daily on Twitter by certain alt-right white supremacist Donald Trump supporters labeling me a "cuck" -- a weak-kneed leftist who wants to watch his wife copulate with a black man. Prominent Breitbart News columnist Milo Yiannopoulos tweeted a picture of a black child at me upon my announcement of the birth of my second child. The neo-Nazi Daily Stormer routinely attacks me. Some of Trump's alt-right fans tweeted that I, along with my wife and two children, should be sent to the gas chambers.

This is the toxicity of our extreme politics. The campus left, enthused by Sen. Bernie Sanders and sought by Hillary Clinton, calls anyone who disagrees a "neo-KKK member." The KKK, meanwhile, calls anyone who won't support Donald Trump a "cuck." This is what happens when basic American principles are no longer taught; this is what happens when grievance politics replace the principles of the Declaration of Independence and the Constitution of the United States of America. Speaking in favor of free speech makes you a pariah for those who would control speech in order to build their utopia.

So, what about those of us who despise both the KKK and the Black Lives Matter movement? What about those of us who think that white nationalism is despicable, and that the censorious brutality of the "diversity" clique is gross? We've got a long road ahead of us. We'll have to teach a new generation, from scratch, that freedom and liberty still matter, regardless of race. We'll have to attempt to restore the notion of a social fabric, rather than the tribalism that now dominates the conversation. We'll have to stand tall against authoritarianism from both sides.

The Left's Mobocracy

June 8, 2016

For years, the left has been desperate to paint conservatives as the real danger to civil society. Back in 2009, the U.S. Department of Homeland Security called conservatives a threat to safety. In a report, it stated that those who oppose abortion and illegal immigration represent a serious domestic terror threat. After presumptive Republican presidential nominee Donald Trump reprehensibly justified violence against protesters, the media was awash with fears that conservatives would suddenly lose their minds and begin brandishing pitchforks in search of unlucky transgender individuals.

But, for decades, the only real threat of mob violence has come from the political left.

The left proved this once again this week when rioters in San Jose, California ignored do-nothing police officers and assaulted Trump supporters after his campaign rally. They overran police barriers, punched random rallygoers and egged a woman. They spit on people, burned American flags and generally made a violent nuisance of themselves.

The left reacted by blaming Trump.

First off, let's point out that while Trump has encouraged his own rallygoers to participate in violence against peaceful protesters, there has *never* been a pro-Trump mob or riot. Individuals have engaged in bad behavior, but there has never been any mass activity. The same is not true of the political left, which traffics in mob action, from Ferguson, Missouri, to Baltimore, Maryland, to Seattle, Washington, to Occupy Wall Street.

Why? Because when conservatives act badly, they're condemned by both conservatives and leftists. But when leftists riot, leftists simply blame conservatives for the riots.

That's what happened in San Jose.

San Jose Mayor Sam Liccardo said, "At some point, Donald Trump needs to take responsibility for the irresponsible behavior of his campaign." San Jose police Chief Eddie Garcia praised his officers for failing to intervene, saying, "We are not an 'occupying force' and cannot reflect the chaotic tactics of protesters." The San Jose Police Department added that it did not intervene so as to not "further (incite) the crowd and produce more violent behavior."

Presumptive Democratic presidential nominee Hillary Clinton blamed Trump, too: "He created an environment in which it seemed to be acceptable for someone running for president to be inciting violence, to be encouraging his supporters. Now we're seeing people who are against him responding in kind." The internet blogging service Vox was forced to suspend editor Emmett Rensin after telling people to "start a riot" if Trump sets foot in their town.

Trump may be a gross thug individually, but conservatives are generally uninterested in the sort of thuggish hordes that roam the streets looking for skulls to crack. We don't like those sorts of folks; we find them an affront to law and order and clean living.

The left has no such compunction. And so long as their leading lights continue to justify such lawlessness in the name of stopping the rhetoric of the right, we're doomed to more broken eggs, broken noses and broken politics.

Yes, it Matters to Say 'Radical Islam'

June 15, 2016

President Obama took to the microphones on Tuesday to rant about the great evil facing Western civilization: Donald Trump's insistence that Obama use the phrase "radical Islam" in describing a radical Muslim's killing of 49 Americans at a gay club in Orlando, Florida. Obama's original comment on the attack consisted of some platitudes about gun control and some happy talk about "various extremist information that was disseminated over the internet." You know, like in those rogue "Teenage Mutant Ninja Turtles" chat rooms.

After Trump slapped Obama for failing to use the phrase "radical Islam," Obama, clearly disturbed, lashed out: "That's the key, they tell us. We can't beat ISIL unless we call them 'radical Islamists.' What exactly would using this label accomplish? What exactly would it change? Would it make ISIL less committed to trying to kill Americans? Would it bring in more allies? Is there a military strategy that is served by this? The answer is: none of the above. Calling a threat by a different name does not make it go away. This is a political distraction." He added: "There is no magic to the phrase 'radical Islam.' It's a political talking point; it's not a strategy."

If it's a political distraction, why not just do it?

If it's a talking point that bothers millions of Americans, why not just use it?

If words mean nothing, why not just say them?

Because Obama knows that the words "radical Islam" mean something. And he doesn't like what they mean.

The words "radical Islam" don't mean -- contrary to his straw man -- that all Muslims are terrorists, or that Muslims will run to terrorism out of fear of the very term "radical Islam." As Andrew

McCarthy rightly points out on National Review: "our enemies despise us and do not judge themselves by how we talk about them. At best, they are indifferent to our language; otherwise, they are so hostile that they mock our 'progressive' obsession over it."

And the words "radical Islam" are not a substitute for strategy, obviously. Hillary Clinton said "radical Islamism" this week, and then said that she'd essentially maintain Obama's Middle East strategy that led to the rise of ISIS and its regional growth and international spread.

What the words "radical Islam" *do* say is that religious ideology matters -- that certain world problems can't be solved by appeal to transnational redistributionism or deliberate attempts to curb American power in favor of great equality among civilizations. Obama thinks that if he ignores the religious ideology of our enemies, they'll come around so long as we pull back and then offer them material goods. That's why his very own State Department suggested that ISIS be given jobs.

But they won't. That's what the phrase "radical Islam" recognizes: The only way to bring people back from the brink is a religious transformation. And that's a pretty serious problem, since people hold their religious beliefs far more closely than any other belief system. It means that it's not enough for a few fringe Muslims to condemn terrorism. It means true reformation, of the sort proposed by Egyptian leader General Abdel-Fattah el-Sissi, not wishful thinking about the current state of the Muslim world, which is replete with fundamentalism that provides impetus to radical Islamic movements.

And *that's* why Obama won't say the phrase. To say it would be to recognize a problem he wishes didn't exist, a problem that undercuts his entire worldview.

And so more Americans will die. The left will babble on endlessly about Islamophobia and gun control while ignoring the only worthwhile goal in a war on radical Islam: the destruction of radical Islam itself.

The Truth Has Been (Omitted)

June 22, 2016

Barack Obama is a dramatic failure.

His economy has been a slow-motion train wreck. His domestic policy has driven racial antagonism to renewed heights and divided Americans from each other along lines of religion and sexual orientation. On foreign policy he has set the world aflame in the name of pretty, meaningless verbiage and a less hegemonic America.

But there's good news: At least he controls the information flow.

This week, Attorney General Loretta Lynch told Americans to believe her rather than their own lying eyes. First, she openly admitted that the FBI would censor the 911 phone call of the jihadi Omar Mateen who murdered 49 Americans at a gay nightclub in Orlando, Florida. The FBI, she said, would remove explicit references to ISIS, ISIS leader Abu Bakr al-Baghdadi and Islam.

The resulting transcript was a masterpiece of hilarious redaction. Here's just a taste: "In the name of God the Merciful, the beneficial (in Arabic) ... Praise be to God, and prayers as well as peace be upon the prophet of (in Arabic). I let you know, I'm in Orlando and I did the shootings. ... My name is I pledge of allegiance to (omitted). ... I pledge allegiance to (omitted), may God protect him (in Arabic) on behalf (omitted)."

This memory holing would make George Orwell cry. In this iteration, Allah becomes God (See, Islam is just like Judaism and Christianity!), but we can't mention terrorist groups and their leaders. In fact, more than a week after the attack, Lynch told the press she didn't know the jihadi's motivation -- a motivation *clearly stated* in the transcript she released.

Insanity.

But this is not unusual for the Obama administration. We know that in the run-up to the Iran deal the Obama administration simply altered reality to fit its narrative: It had fiction writer and deputy national security advisor Ben Rhodes cook up an account where negotiations with the terror state began only after the accession of "moderate" President Hassan Rouhani. Never mind that Obama and company had been negotiating with the mullahs behind the scenes for years before that. The narrative had to be falsified and upheld. When the State Department was forced to admit those lies in a press conference, the White House conveniently chopped out that section of the taped conference for public release.

We also know that the Obama administration lied openly about Obamacare. It knew from the beginning that you couldn't keep your doctor or your plan. It simply hid that fact for years. We know that the Obama State Department sliced out a section of transcript mentioning radical Islam when French President Francois Hollande visited the United States.

He who controls the information flow controls reality.

And the Obama administration is already rewriting reality for the historians of decades hence. We won't find out where they hid most of the political bodies until too late -- just as we won't find out what Clinton hid in her private server until far too late.

This is why a government must not be trusted with massive power. Politicians have every incentive not just to lie in the present but to lie with an eye toward the future. The more power they have over us, the more power they have over the reality we see -- and the more they think they can get away with manipulating that reality.

When Abortion Fans Let the
Truth Slip out

June 29, 2016

On Monday, the Supreme Court issued yet another politically driven leftist decision, this time over the contentious issue of abortion. The court explained that not only did the Constitution of the United States mandate that states not infringe upon the phantom right to abortion but that health regulations on abortion clinics in Texas had to be overturned if they made it less convenient for women to kill their babies at such clinics.

To this decision, "The Daily Show" had but one well-considered response: "Celebrate the #SCOTUS ruling! Go knock someone up in Texas!"

The right reacted without outrage; even the left found the tweet sufficiently indiscreet to merit a bit of tut-tutting.

The left shouldn't have bothered. The left's old abortion position -- "safe, legal and rare" -- never made any logical sense. If abortion kills a human child, then it shouldn't be legal. If abortion kills a nonhuman, it shouldn't be rare. Nobody cares about whether polyp removals are rare. The left fully believes that abortion is merely another form of birth control. I saw this firsthand in 2012 at the Democratic National Convention in Charlotte, North Carolina. Young men walked around wearing buttons reading "I LOVE PRO-CHOICE WOMEN."

Of course they do.

In fact, abortion as birth control is implicit in their new set of revisions to the Democratic Party platform. The latest version of the DNC document calls for revocation of *all* restrictions on abortion at the state and federal levels -- yes, all, including partial-birth abortion, the gruesome procedure in which late-term children are carved up in the womb. They want you to fund abortions, too, both at home and abroad.

That's not "safe, legal and rare." That's "let's kill as many babies as we want."

And Hillary Clinton agrees with all of this. On Monday, she tweeted: "This fight isn't over: The next president has to protect women's health. Women won't be 'punished' for exercising their basic rights." Babies are not a punishment; they're a gift. But Clinton believes babies are only a gift if the mother decides that she wants it. Otherwise the baby is merely a collection of cells.

Defining what constitutes life based on convenience is the height of evil. Slaveholders in the South did precisely that in the antebellum era, arguing that blacks living below the Mason-Dixon Line were property. What business was it of those nosey parkers in Boston, Massachusetts, what a plantation owner in South Carolina thought of his slaves? The Nazis did that to Jews; Jews were subhuman, and therefore unfit for human treatment. The Hutus did it to the Tutsis. ISIS does it to Yazidis. The essence of inhumanity lies in the purposeful dehumanization of other human beings.

That is what the Democratic Party does explicitly. Democrats only get embarrassed when someone on their own side is uncouth enough to admit it publicly.

Hillary Clinton: Too Big to Jail

July 6, 2016

On Monday America celebrated the 240th anniversary of the adoption of the Declaration of Independence, which condemned King George III for "(obstructing) the Administration of Justice." On Tuesday the American left celebrated as the federal government obstructed the administration of justice on behalf of one of its ruling families, the Clintons.

Last week the attorney general of the United States met with former President Bill Clinton, whose wife and foundation were under FBI investigation. They both insisted nothing untoward happened. Days later The New York Times reported that Hillary Clinton might offer Lynch a position in her administration.

Over the holiday weekend the Obama administration announced that President Obama would fly to North Carolina with Clinton aboard Air Force One in order to campaign with her. Americans would, in part, foot the bill for the travel.

On Tuesday FBI Director James Comey called a supposedly impromptu press conference to announce his findings in the investigation of Clinton's private email server. He began by announcing that nobody knew what he was about to say, which seems implausible given that Obama was preparing to go onstage with Clinton at the time. Is it even within the realm of imagination that Obama would stand next to Clinton hours after Comey announced the intent to prosecute her? Of course not.

Then, Comey proceeded to lay out all the reasons why Clinton should have been indicted: She set up multiple private email servers, all of which were vulnerable to hack; she did not set them up in order to use one mobile device, as she has so often stated; she transmitted and received highly classified material; her team deleted emails that could have contained relevant and classified information; she knew that classified information was crossing her server. He concluded that Clinton's team was "extremely careless in their handling of very sensitive, highly classified information."

This was all criminal activity.

But Clinton is a member of the Royal Family. Thus, said Comey, she was innocent. Comey tried to say he wouldn't recommend prosecution because she didn't have the requisite intent, but the law doesn't *require* intent; it requires merely "gross negligence" under 18 U.S.C. 793. In fact, even the level of intent required to charge under statutes like 18 U.S.C. 1924 and 18 U.S.C. 798 was clearly met: the intent to place classified information in a nonapproved, non-classified place.

Nonetheless, Clinton would be allowed to roam free -- and become president. "To be clear," Comey intoned, "this is not to suggest that in similar circumstances, a person who engaged in this activity would face no consequences. To the contrary, those individuals are often subject to security or administrative sanctions. But that is not what we are deciding now."

One rule for the peons, one for the potentates.

This is the Wilsonian legacy, finally achieved after a century of waiting: the Big Man (or Woman), unanswerable to the law, approved by the population without regard to equality under the law. We now elect our dictators. And they are unanswerable to us -- except, presumably, once every four years. The commonfolk, on the other hand, find themselves on the wrong side of the government gun every day.

Tyranny doesn't start with jackboots. It begins with the notion that a different law applies to the powerful than to the powerless. Under Barack Obama tyranny has become a way of life. Ronald Reagan always said that freedom was one generation away from extinction. It looks like we've finally found that generation.

For Obama, Leftist Rhetoric Is Always Innocent and Conservatives Are Always Guilty

July 13, 2016

When it comes to the linkage between violence and rhetoric, I abide by a fairly simple rule: If you're not advocating violence, you're not responsible for violence. That doesn't mean your rhetoric is decent or appropriate; it may be vile, awful and factually incorrect. But it isn't the cause for violence.

President Barack Obama also abides by a simple rule when it comes to linking violence and rhetoric: If he doesn't like the rhetoric, it's responsible for violence. And if there's violence associated with rhetoric he likes, then the violence must have been caused by something else.

This shining double standard was on full display this week after an anti-white racist black man shot 14 police officers in Dallas just hours after Obama appeared on national television explaining that alleged instances of police brutality and racism were "not isolated incidents" but rather "symptomatic of a broader set of racial disparities that exist in our criminal justice system." Obama was happy to label the shootings of Alton Sterling in Louisiana and Philando Castile in Minnesota, without evidence, as part of a broader racist trend in law enforcement across the country.

Then Micah Xavier Johnson opened fire on white police officers -- and anti-police racist radicals attacked officers in Minnesota, Tennessee, Missouri, Georgia and Texas again -- and Obama suddenly got amnesia. Now, it turned out, rhetoric had nothing to do with their actions. In fact, said Obama, he had no idea why Johnson -- who explicitly said he wanted to murder white cops -- would do such a thing. "I think it's very hard to untangle the motives of this shooter," Obama said while in Poland. "What triggers that, what feeds it, what sets it off -- I'll leave that to psychologists and people who study these kinds of incidents." He did blame one element for the attack, however: lack of gun control. "If you care about the safety of our police officers," he lied, "you can't set aside the gun issue and pretend that that's irrelevant."

Odd how this works. When a white racist shoots up a black church in Charleston, South Carolina, Obama targets America's legacy of racism, and the entire media call for a national fight against Confederate flags; when a nut tries to shoot up a Planned Parenthood building in Colorado, the left emerges to claim that the pro-life movement bears culpability. But when an Orlando jihadi shoots up a gay nightclub, Obama and company declare the motives totally mysterious and then impugn Christian social conservatives and the National Rifle Association.

Here's the truth: Obama's rhetoric isn't responsible for murder, but it's certainly responsible for death. That's because Obama's racist rhetoric has led to the greatest rise in racial polarization since the 1970s. In 2010, just 13 percent of Americans worried about race relations, whereas in April 2016, 35 percent of Americans did. That racial polarization has, in turn, led to distrust of police officers, many of whom respond by pulling out of the communities that need their help most. Crime rates go up, including murder rates. Ironically, Obama's supposed rage at white officers killing blacks leads to more blacks killing blacks in cities no longer policed by whites.

But there's good news: Obama can always blame everyone else. When you're held responsible for your feelings rather than your actions, it's always simple to direct attention toward the evil conservatives who insist that all lives matter rather than care enough about black lives to save them by endorsing the police who work to protect black men and women every day.

When Do Values Trump Democracy?

July 20, 2016

Last Friday, a splinter of the powerful Turkish military attempted a coup against President Recep Tayyip Erdogan, an Islamist with a taste for the authoritarian. Erdogan has spent the past decade purging the military of secularists and integrating his own brand of radical Islam into government; in the process, he's also accrued a $182 million fortune and three palaces, including a $650 million Saddam-esque monstrosity. He's cracked down on journalists, gone soft on the Islamic State group and threatened to get rid of the constitutional court. He is, in short, an aspiring dictator.

The coup, unfortunately, failed.

Or perhaps the coup was a setup. Erdogan has used the failure of the coup as an excuse to completely purge his enemies. He has demanded that the United States hand over a moderate cleric he sees as his enemy; he has detained or suspended 20,000 police, civil service, judiciary and army members; he has called to reinstate the death penalty for those who attempted the coup; 1,500 finance ministry officials were thrown out; and 30 governors were fired, as well.

In response, U.S. Secretary of State John Kerry blustered, "NATO ... has a requirement with respect to democracy." Given that the Obama administration stood by and did nothing after Syrian dictator Bashar Assad used chemical weapons on his own citizens, Erdogan probably laughed out loud at this missive.

So, was the coup moral?

Some on the left say no. A columnist for The Guardian, Owen Jones, tweeted: "You don't have to support Turkey's government. An attack on democracy is an attack on democracy everywhere." Except, of course, that it isn't. An attempted coup against Adolf

Hitler, who became chancellor of Germany legitimately in 1932, or against Benito Mussolini, who became prime minister of Italy through democratic means in 1922, would have been fully justified. Today a coup against the "elected" government in Iran would be similarly decent, as would a coup against the "elected" government in Hamas-controlled Gaza.

For well over a century, the left has mistaken the means of democracy for democratic values. That confusion has converted republics into tyrannies. Just because people elect their dictators doesn't make the dictators legitimate. This is the whole point of the Constitution of the United States. There are certain rights that are inviolable, even by a majority. If a majority voted to enslave a minority, according to Jones' logic, a coup would be illegitimate; after all, that would be overturning the popular will. That, presumably, is why he is a socialist. For him, morality follows the majority.

But morality doesn't follow the majority. Democracy and classical liberalism should go hand in hand, but they don't always; a people trained in classical liberalism will vote for it, but a people trained in tyranny will vote for tyranny. That's what's been happening in Turkey. Increasingly, it's what's happening everywhere.

Values must trump democracy if the two come into conflict. They don't have to. But it's our job to educate our children and, indeed, populations around the world about the meaning of classical liberal values. If we don't, people will choose their own chains. And just because you choose your chains doesn't mean those chains are somehow any less oppressive.

When Americans Want to Elect Mommy or Daddy

July 27, 2016

Americans want to elect Daddy or Mommy.

That's what this election has become. It hasn't been about competing or contrasting visions of government. It hasn't been about rooting out corruption in Washington or bringing change to the system. It certainly hasn't been about principle.

No, this election has become a simple decision: Do you want the thickheaded loudmouth who understands your problems, or do you want the cold and calculating robotic manipulator who doesn't? Do you want the real-life Archie Bunker, or would you prefer Mary Tyler Moore in "Ordinary People"?

That's what the latest polls tell us. They tell us that Americans aren't happy with either of their choices. Fully 45 percent of Democrats wish someone other than Hillary Clinton had won the primary, and the same percentage of Republicans wish someone other than Donald Trump had been nominated. Sixty-eight percent of Americans think Clinton isn't honest or trustworthy; 54 percent think she's running for personal gain rather than the good of the country; 57 percent say Clinton would divide the country as president; and just 38 percent say they'd be proud to have her as president. Trump's numbers are bad, too, but he has a significant advantage on honesty (with 55 percent saying he's dishonest). Forty-seven percent say he's running for personal gain, and 55 percent say he'd divide the country as president.

Trump is now beating Clinton where it counts. People believe that he understands their problems and believe that Clinton doesn't.

Here's the bigger problem, however: Electing politicians who "understand your problems" is a recipe for disaster. Governing properly isn't about identifying with the feelings of constituents; that position logically leads to a politics of individual "problem-solving" focused solely on curing constituents' ills. Governing properly should be about understanding that government's job *isn't* to solve Americans' problems; it's about moving aside obstacles so that Americans can solve their own problems.

No longer.

Bill Clinton is truly the father of the "feel your pain" politics, the notion that politicians ought to be beer buddies, folks who get what we feel and respond to it. This is a successful campaign strategy, but it changes what we're looking for. Now we're looking for candidates who can demonstrate that they get us and candidates who can provide for us. We're looking for President Benjamin Spock.

But government is not our parent. Though comedian Chris Rock may think that Barack Obama is the "dad of the country," he most certainly isn't. And if we think of our presidents that way, we're likely to stop holding them accountable. Even children of abusive parents love their parents. And even when nearly 7 in 10 Americans believe that the country is moving in the wrong direction, 56 percent of Americans think President Obama's doing a terrific job.

This means that our government is no longer accountable to us, even in our own minds. Government just becomes a popularity contest rather than a tool for the protection of rights. And our presidents become our parents; our parents become our dictators; and our dictators become unanswerable. It's comforting to think that politicians care about you, but they're lying. They don't. They care about themselves. And to project daddy and mommy issues onto those we elect is to hand over our God-given rights for the cheap promises of baby kissers.

Trump Simply Can't Stop Himself

August 3, 2016

This week, Donald Trump decided to step on every rake in a 30-mile radius. Fresh off of Hillary Clinton's pathetic display of insanely soporific robotics -- she really is remarkably lifelike for an evil cyborg sent from the future to kill Sarah Connor -- Trump decided to redirect the news cycle. He did so by attacking a Gold Star family who spoke at the Democratic National Convention.

After the Khan family excoriated Trump for his proposed Muslim immigration ban by speaking in emotional terms about their slain son, Capt. Humayun Khan, Trump couldn't stop himself. He fired back. He did so by questioning why the mother, Ghazala Khan, hadn't spoken out, implying strongly that her religion prevented her from doing so. He then said that he has made sacrifices akin to those made by the Khan family.

Forget right or wrong (and this was wrong). This is idiotic.

But Trump can't stop himself. If there's one baseline character trait that makes Trump Trump it's his utter inability to stop himself from hitting back. The Clinton campaign could run a puppy across a Trump stage wearing an "I'm With Her" collar, and Trump would find himself punting it and then telling the media the puppy had it coming.

This, of course, is precisely what animated many conservatives to vote for Trump in the first place. They watched him knock Jeb! Bush through a wall repeatedly and figured that he'd do the same with Clinton -- he'd hit her with the kitchen sink, then grab the bathroom sink and hit her again.

Unfortunately, Trump's willingness to hit back provides him with an almost infinite number of targets. When you're a presidential candidate, you're on everybody's mind for months at a time. Many of those people will say negative things about you. If you're going to run after every squirrel, you'll find yourself both tired and behind in the race.

But that's Trump.

And his supporters continue to convince themselves that this is smart. For months, now, they've been suggesting that Trump will somehow right the ship, that he's playing 19-dimensional chess. They shout that Trump's opponents should shut up and jump on the Trump Train. And so, Trump keeps being Trump. After all, what incentive does he have to change? He'll always have his base, and it will continue to cheer him along. And because Trump is motivated by praise and criticism, he'll react to it.

Trump's supporters were a cheap date. Unwilling to condemn Trump's morally asinine comments, willing to follow Trump down every rabbit hole, they've actually made Trump a *weaker* candidate. That's why Clinton, the weakest major party candidate of my lifetime, is now destroying Trump in the polls. Somehow, Trump is finding a way to lose to a living embodiment of corruption and nastiness.

Can Trump turn it around? That's unlikely. After all, that would require him to turn his back on the squirrels and focus on his actual opponents. He'd have to stop obsessing about Ted Cruz and worry about Hillary Clinton. He'd have to leave the Khan family alone and focus on President Obama. He'd have to stop being Donald Trump.

And Trump will always be Trump.

No, Barack Obama Isn't a Feminist -- He's a Self-Aggrandizing Tool

August 10, 2016

This week, President Obama penned a ridiculous piece in Glamour magazine. It dripped with self-regard and oozed with moral preening. Barack Obama, said Barack Obama, is a true feminist. This, of course, might not have been obvious from the fact that the Obama White House has paid women 89 cents for every dollar earned by a man, as of July. It might not have been obvious from the Obama administration's belief that even men can be women, so long as they think it so -- and they can invade women's bathrooms, based on that subjective belief.

But Obama, said Obama, is indeed a feminist.

And he is also here to change souls. "The most important change," he lectured, "may be the toughest of all -- and that's changing ourselves."

How should Americans change themselves? Obama explained: "We need to keep changing the attitude that permits the routine harassment of women, whether they're walking down the street or daring to go online. We need to keep changing the attitude that teaches men to feel threatened by the presence and success of women."

This sort of unearned moral righteousness induces nausea. Notice that Obama doesn't offer any solutions to these supposedly widespread problems -- he just throws out the notion that he *understands* women's problems. To borrow some feminist language, that's an extraordinarily patriarchal attitude -- to condescend to tell women that you *understand* their problems and therefore need not present solutions. As the subtext goes, all women really want is someone who can *feel* along with them.

But it's worse than that. According to Obama, "We need to keep changing the attitude that punishes women for their sexuality and rewards men for theirs." But why should anyone be rewarded for their sexuality? Do we reward people for other bodily functions and choices? Do we reward people for their eating habits? How about their bowel movements? The only sort of sexuality that society should celebrate is the kind that takes place responsibly within the bounds of marriage, given that if sexuality produces children, we want children to be born into solid, two-parent families, with their parents present. Society should be -- at best -- neutral about other sorts of sexuality. It seems bizarre that feminism should ask for promiscuity to be treated as virtue for women just because bad people have done so for men.

This stuff isn't feminism. It's just politically correct virtue-signaling.

I fully believe in the basic notion of original feminism: that women should be able to make whatever career choices they want, based on merit. I grew up in a home in which my dad was a stay-at-home dad and my mom ran television and film companies. My wife is a doctor. I'm certainly at home with the kids more than she is, but she took time off for both of our kids. I want my daughter to be able to pursue whatever dream she sees fit.

But I don't believe that America's soul needs changing. That's because I know that Americans agree with me. If they didn't, my mom's career wouldn't have been possible, and neither would my wife's. I don't spend every day worrying about my daughter's possibilities, because in a free country she can go as far as her skills and decisions take her. If she faces obstacles from sexists, I'll be right there calling for action, if she wants my help. But I'm not going to pretend for the sake of political correctness and popularity that sexism is widespread and pervasive. It isn't. America is a glorious place for women, and the only way to make it even better is to target actual sexist activity, to stop slandering men as sexists without evidence and to tell our daughters that there are no glass ceilings, just a world of options waiting for them.

After all, that happens to be the truth.

Trump Isn't an Easy Decision, and Nobody Should Pretend He Is

August 17, 2016

Serious acrimony has now broken out among conservatives regarding whether to vote for Donald Trump.

As I've made clear, as of now I have no intention to vote for Trump. He's personally unpalatable, of course -- a serial adulterer who brags about sleeping with married women and says doesn't repent, an extreme narcissist with delusions of grandeur. He's not conservative. He thinks Planned Parenthood does wonderful work, he has no coherent foreign policy, he wants to leave entitlement programs in place, he supports tariffs and government subsidies, he doesn't care if Republicans lose the Senate and he has nothing to say about religious freedom for business owners, among a myriad of other policy shortcomings. He's volatile and nasty. He has mocked prisoners of war and a disabled journalist, compared his own sacrifices to those of Gold Star families and gone soft on the Ku Klux Klan. He lies constantly, about nearly everything.

Just as importantly, Trump is doing serious brand damage to conservatism. He's poisoning the well with female voters, minorities and young people. Many ardent conservatives have been co-opted into lying for him and perverting their own conservatism in order to stop Hillary Clinton. If Trump wins, he'll turn conservatism into Trumpism; if he loses and conservatives go along for the ride, he'll have sunk conservatism for an entire generation of voters.

Not supporting Trump is a perfectly defensible position, but it's a tough call.

On the other hand, I fully understand and sympathize with the position of those who say they must hold their nose and vote for

Trump in order to stop Clinton. She'll be a full-scale disaster. She'll appoint a fifth Supreme Court justice to gut the First and Second Amendments. She'll cripple our military. She'll cram down tax increases and use the regulatory infrastructure to snap the knees of American industry.

Choosing Trump over Clinton is a perfectly defensible position, but it's a tough call.

Each morning these days, I ask myself the same question: Which is more costly to America, a possible loss of conservatism to Trumpist, nationalist populism and all its attendant lying, which could forever prevent the resurrection of constitutional Republicanism, or another four years of Hillary Clinton's radical destruction, which could deal the deathblow to American freedoms?

This is a serious question, and good people will come down on both sides of it. But acknowledging that the choice isn't easy seems like a stretch for many commentators. Some insist that foregoing the Trump Train makes you a traitor. In order to reach this conclusion, they either ignore Trump's foibles or lie about what a wonderful conservative he is. Some insist that jumping on the Trump Train makes you a traitor. In order to reach this conclusion, they downplay Clinton's evils or exaggerate Trump's riskiness.

It *does* make you a traitor to conservatism to lie for Trump or lie to your audience that he is a serious conservative. Lying isn't just nonconservative. It's plainly immoral. But neither voting for Trump nor refusing to vote for him makes you a traitor.

Nobody knows the answer to the hypothetical I pose to myself each morning, because nobody has a crystal ball. But one thing is certain: If we don't recognize that the choice is tough -- thanks to Trump's utterly incomprehensible foolishness and vitriol and Clinton's radical leftist corruption -- we're not taking the question seriously. More importantly, we're destined to go to war with our own ideological allies after the election is over. And there's no need for that war. Our war should be on behalf of conservatism. Trump has divided conservatives on the proper tactics. But once Nov. 9 hits, we're all on the same page again: We must either stop leftist policies from President Trump or President Clinton. And we'll need to be allies.

The first step should be recognizing the good will of those who fight alongside us, even if we don't make the same risk calculations with regard to a conservative future.

Hillary's Corruption Is Overwhelming

August 24, 2016

After over two decades in the heart of America's spotlight, Hillary Clinton is still an unknown quantity for most Americans. That's thanks to one factor and one factor only: the love and worship of the mainstream media.

Over the weekend, no less than six terrible stories broke that would have crippled anyone else's campaign. First, we learned that Clinton aide and confidante Huma Abedin acted as assistant editor on the radical Journal of Muslim Minority Affairs, where she greenlit pieces that stated that "pushing (mothers) out into the open labor market is a clear demonstration of a lack of respect of womanhood and motherhood," among other things.

Next, we found out that Clinton had blamed former Secretary of State Colin Powell for giving her the idea to set up a private email server at a dinner party, and that Powell not only denied giving her the idea but also denied ever having a dinner conversation with her on the topic. Former Secretary of State Condoleezza Rice, who Clinton claimed was present for the conversation, has also denied the story.

Then we discovered that the Clinton State Department oversaw some $6 billion in mismanagement, fraud and incompetence.

Meanwhile, it was revealed that Clinton's pay-for-play -- Clinton Foundation donations in exchange for access to the State Department -- ran deeper than originally thought.

And we learned that the FBI and Justice Department are investigating the Podesta Group -- co-founded by Clinton campaign chairman John Podesta -- over its ties with former Ukrainian President and Vladimir Putin ally Viktor Yanukovych.

Finally, we found out that the FBI uncovered some 15,000 emails that Clinton failed to disclose to the State Department. Presumably, they do not all concern yoga and Chelsea Clinton's wedding plans.

So, what was the media's response to this tidal wave of incompetence and corruption?

They focused on the Trump campaign's internal mess, naturally. That's what they always do.

And that's why Trump became the Republican nominee.

The media once painted former Gov. Mitt Romney the way they paint Donald Trump, and they excoriated anyone who dared to ask about President Barack Obama's botched Benghazi policy. They scoffed at Romney's suggestion that Obama's Russian policy had emboldened Moscow. They castigated legislators like former Rep. Michele Bachmann for connecting Huma Abedin to Islamic radicalism via the Journal of Muslim Minority Affairs.

By the time Trump came along, the American people had already rejected the media's capacity for truth-telling. So when the media targeted Trump and Trump refused to be cowed by them, many Republicans resonated to Trump's call. They believed that Trump would hit Clinton with all the material the media covered up and ignored.

So far, that hasn't panned out. Trump's been far too distractible to focus on Clinton. But that doesn't mean that he couldn't. If Trump were to target Clinton, he'd be doing the job Americans thought they elected him to do: exposing the empress who's protected by the media Praetorian Guard.

If he doesn't, Clinton will become president, scandals and all. The media are still the gatekeepers, and they still have no intention of allowing Clinton to become the story when Trump's tweets can be.

We Have Nothing Left Holding Us Together

August 31, 2016

On Friday, a South Carolina high school stopped students from bringing American flags to a football game against a heavily Hispanic rival school. Why? The principal was presumably worried that waving the flag might offend the Hispanic students. According to the principal, "This decision would be made anytime that the American flag, or any other symbol, sign, cheer, or action on the part of our fans would potentially compromise the safety of all in attendance at a school event."

This isn't the first such situation. The 9th U.S. Circuit Court of Appeals ruled last year that a public school in California could ban students from wearing a shirt emblazoned with an American flag on Cinco de Mayo thanks to fears over racial conflict at the school. The lawyer for the children complained, "This opens the door for a school to suppress any viewpoints that are opposed by a band of vocal and violent bullies."

Meanwhile, has-been San Francisco 49ers quarterback Colin Kaepernick has been widely praised in the media for refusing to stand for the national anthem during football games. "I am not going to stand up to show pride in a flag for a country that oppresses black people and people of color," explained the man earning an average of $19,000,000 per year for sitting on the bench. He continued: "To me, this is bigger than football and it would be selfish on my part to look the other way. There are bodies in the street and people getting paid leave and getting away with murder."

We're watching the end of America in real time.

That doesn't mean that the country's on the verge of actual implosion. But the idea of America required a common definition of *being* American: a love of country on the basis of its founding philosophy. That has now been undermined by the left.

Love of country doesn't mean that you have to love everything about America, or that you can't criticize America. But loving America means understanding that the country was founded on a unique basis -- a uniquely *good* basis. That's what the flag stands for. Not ethnic superiority or racial solidarity or police brutality but the notion of individual liberty and equal rights before God. But with the destruction of that central principle, the ties that bind us together are fraying. And the left loves that.

In fact, the two defining philosophical iterations of the modern left both make war with the ties that bind us together. In President Obama's landmark second inaugural address, he openly said, "Being true to our founding documents...does not mean we all define liberty in exactly the same way." This is the kind of definition worshipped by Justice Anthony Kennedy, who has singlehandedly redefined the Constitution. He said, "At the heart of liberty is the right to define one's own concept of existence, of meaning, of the universe, and of the mystery of human life."

But this means that liberty has no real definition outside of "stuff I want to do." And we all want to do different stuff, sometimes at the expense of other people's liberty. Subjective definitions of liberty, rather than a common definition, means a conflict of all against all, or at least a conflict of a government controlled by some who are targeting everyone else. It means that our flag is no longer a common symbol for our shared definition of liberty. It's just a rag that means different things to different people based on their subjective experiences and definitions of reality.

And that means we have nothing holding us together.

The only way to restore the ties that bind us is to rededicate ourselves to the notion of liberty for which generations of Americans fought and died. But that won't happen so long as the left insists that their feelings are more important than your rights.

Hillary's Email Scandal Takes Down the FBI

September 7, 2016

For months Americans wondered whether the FBI, led by Director James Comey, would take down the most corrupt woman in the history of American politics, Hillary Clinton.

As it turns out, Hillary Clinton took down the FBI.

According to new documents from the FBI's investigation of Clinton, the agency was fully aware that Clinton lied when she said she set up a private server in order to utilize one Blackberry device -- she used 13 mobile devices and two phone numbers. The FBI knew that Clinton's aides destroyed old Blackberrys by cracking them in half or hitting them with a hammer. The FBI knew full well that Clinton had passed classified information over her private server -- she admitted that she didn't even know how classified information worked, instead stating that she thought the "C" appearing at the top of documents probably had something to do with alphabetizing files. The FBI recognized that Clinton wiped her server after a New York Times article revealed her private sever and email use; that she brought her Blackberry into a secure State Department area; that she never turned over nearly 18,000 work-related emails; that she discussed an undercover asset on the server and put his family in danger; and that she refused to take Blackberrys from the State Department out of fear they could be discoverable under Freedom of Information Act requests.

That's not all.

The FBI also allowed Clinton aide Cheryl Mills to act as Clinton's lawyer during her FBI hearing, even though Mills was a material witness. In doing so, the agency granted Mills legal privilege where none existed. And the FBI didn't bother asking Clinton whether she intended to hide information. Officials gave her the benefit of the doubt every single step of the way.

And then the FBI recommended to the Department of Justice that she not be indicted.

The fix was in.

The press seems sanguine about the possibility of Clinton in the White House. That's bizarre given her corruption. It's even more bizarre when you consider that she has now undermined Americans' trust in the chief domestic intelligence agency in the country, making it a laughingstock and a political Hackey Sack. Director Comey entered this investigation well-liked and well-respected across the political aisle. He will exit having destroyed his reputation for honesty on the shoals of Clinton's lies.

There is no excuse for Clinton escaping charges. Not one. The FBI's own documents prove that she took action that you would only take if you were attempting to obstruct justice, destroy evidence and lie to law enforcement. And yet the FBI, as a wing of the Obama White House, went out of its way to ensure that the Democratic presidential candidate would evade prosecution. That means it lacks basic legitimacy.

It's not the only agency the Obama administration has exposed as a political hammer. It has corrupted the Internal Revenue Service, the Department of Justice, the Environmental Protection Agency, the State Department and the Department of Health and Human Services. The list is nearly endless. No wonder so many Americans seem willing to turn to a man who promises to burn the entire structure down, Donald Trump. There's little worth saving here, unless you're a Democrat hoping to uphold the integrity of institutions dedicated to preserving scandal-ridden Democrats.

Hillary Clinton Sees Her Own Voters As the 47 Percent

September 14, 2016

How many times must the left tell Americans what it thinks of them before Americans realize a simple fact: Leftist leaders simply don't like half the country? In 2012, the media lost its mind over former Gov. Mitt Romney's statement that 47 percent of Americans "who are dependent upon government, who believe that they are victims, who believe the government has a responsibility to care for them" would vote for President Obama. This apparently demonstrated that Romney hates everyday Americans. Disdains them. Sees them as moochers.

In 2008, then-Sen. Barack Obama claimed that small-town Americans in the Midwest are benighted hicks. "It's not surprising then they get bitter, they cling to guns or religion or antipathy toward people who aren't like them or anti-immigrant sentiment or anti-trade sentiment as a way to explain their frustrations," he said. This received attention from the conservative press, but was downplayed by the mainstream media, or brushed off as accurate.

This weekend, Hillary Clinton echoed Obama. She said: "To just be grossly generalistic, you could put half of Trump's supporters into what I call the basket of deplorables. Right? The racist, sexist, homophobic, xenophobic, Islamophobic -- you name it. And unfortunately there are people like that." The other half of Trump supporters, Clinton said, are little better: "But that other basket of people are people who feel that the government has let them down, the economy has let them down, nobody cares about them, nobody worries about what happens to their lives and their futures, and they're just desperate for change. ... Those are people we have to understand and empathize with as well."

Clinton's language is far more telling than Obama's. Democrats routinely see voters they don't understand as morally deficient. That provides them the comforting illusion that disagreement reflects lack of virtue. And that means that their policies need not succeed -- success or failure is irrelevant to the ethical question of how to vote. Good people will vote for them regardless of track record, while bad people will oppose them.

But Clinton's language goes further. Where Obama simply labels his opponents as bad guys, Clinton suggests that Romney was right: Those who are her potential supporters are pathetic losers waiting for government to save them. They are disappointed with the economy. They think the government must do more. They just need some tender, loving care from Clinton, and then they'll realize that Trump isn't the man for them.

This means that the sneering tone so many people detected in Romney exists among Democrats *for their own constituents*. Clinton doesn't label her potential voters self-sufficient Americans seeking an equal opportunity. No. They're grievance-mongers, ne'er-do-wells and people who believe they are victims, who believe government has an obligation to take care of them. And she thinks she can draw them to the Democratic Party.

So, where are all the good Americans? To Democrats they don't exist. There are just the deplorables and the needies -- and the elites who control them. *That's* the scariest thing about the Clinton vision for America. Nobody deserves freedom because nobody wants freedom. Everyone is either a racist or in need of saving; everyone needs a cure, either of their soul or their material well-being. And Clinton thinks she can provide that cure, by crushing half of Trump's supporters and co-opting the other half.

She's only missing one thing: Most Trump supporters, and most Americans, aren't bitter clingers or victims. They're independent human beings, waiting for a candidate who wants to grant them that independence -- if any elite is willing to stand up for it.

What to Expect in the First Debate

September 20, 2016

Thanks to the nomination of volatile reality television star Donald Trump, the first presidential debate between Trump and the soporific Hillary Clinton is widely expected to draw record numbers. With the polls knotted up and the swing states in heavy contention, conventional wisdom says that the debate will be exciting, a bloodletting between the staid Clinton and the aggressive Trump.

But actually, it could be massively boring.

Right now, Trump's agenda is simple: appear sane. Clinton has been attempting, somewhat successfully, to portray Trump as an escapee from a mental hospital, a madman on the loose, a man who would unleash nuclear war if handed the keys to the nuclear arsenal. In the past few weeks, Trump's campaign manager, Kellyanne Conway, has apparently been able to get Trump under control. Like a pent-up movie monster chained to the wall of a dank dungeon, Trump's aggression waits -- lurks. But it has not reappeared since Trump's infamous attack on the gold star Khan family. Every so often, we've seen flashes of Crazy Trump (Vladimir Putin's a great guy! Do we really know whether Obama was born in the United States?). But he's been sticking to the teleprompter onstage and avoiding press scrums offstage. The man who once criticized Clinton for avoiding a press conference for well over 200 days has now gone over 50 days without a presser. Real Donald Trump is in hiding, @realdonaldtrump has been handed over to a blind trust, and Teleprompter Trump is on the loose.

That means that Clinton's task during the first debate will be to break into the dungeon and free the monster. To that end, The New York Times reports that Clinton has been speaking with psychologists to explore where she can poke Trump, in order to prompt him to turn into the Hulk -- complete with purple pants. According to the Times, "They are undertaking a forensic-style analysis of Mr. Trump's performances in the Republican primary debates, cataloging strengths and weaknesses as well as trigger points that caused him to lash out in less-than-presidential ways."

Trump's task: Avoid those pitfalls, take six Valium, and wake up president.

Meanwhile, Clinton's main goal will be to appear lifelike. With questions swirling around her health and stamina, she'll be expected to flash energy and wit. She'll also be expected to not appear as a complete liar, which is an uphill task -- it's far easier for a seemingly crazy person to appear stable (every Hollywood actor) than for a serial liar to appear honest. She's got an uphill battle, but she'll mostly want to avoid controversy from Trump.

This means that the debate will come to whether Trump can avoid being portrayed as a character from "One Flew Over The Cuckoo's Nest," and whether Clinton can avoid being portrayed as the title player from "Weekend at Bernie's."

Sounds riveting.

This is what happens when the standards for our politicians finally hit rock bottom: We end up with a discussion between a guy who simply needs to act like a normal person and a woman who simply needs to act like a warm body. It would serve Americans right that after selecting candidates for entertainment value they end up with the season finale of "Joe Millionaire."

Excuses for Losing Just Don't Cut It

September 28, 2016

When Mitt Romney lost in 2012, there was very little discussion of blame. Everyone assumed that Romney simply lost because he didn't do a good enough job of convincing voters to punch the ballot for him. He didn't debate Barack Obama properly; he didn't stand up to Candy Crowley; he backed off of the Benghazi issue, or botched it completely; he gratuitously insulted 47 percent of Americans.

Romney lost, Republicans generally believed, because Romney deserved to lose -- even if he deserved to win morally.

That's not so for Donald Trump.

Never has a presidential candidate had so many ready-made excuses for his mess of a campaign. Since the primaries, Trump's defenders have justified his every gaffe by saying, "Well, he's just a businessman!" His anti-conservative heresies have been excused with a wave of the hand and a comment of, "Well, conservatism has never accomplished anything, anyway!" His general ignorance with regard to basic issues has been shrugged away: "He's learning!" His general unpopularity has been attributed not to his own narcissistic nastiness but to an unnamed group of conspirators out to get him. Sometimes, it's the eeeeevil "cuck" Never Trumpers hiding in their holes, waiting to strike him down at any moment. Sometimes, it's the Machiavellian "establishment" seeking to crush this supposed change agent. And sometimes, it's a suspiciously defective earpiece forcing him to go soft on David Duke and the Ku Klux Klan.

Now, after his airplane vomit bag of a debate performance -- a performance in which he spent the first 30 minutes bloodying Hillary Clinton, only to revert to insecure, incoherent defenses of birtherism, his business record and his Iraq war opposition -- Trump has a whole new set of excuses.

First, Trump's defenders attack his microphone. Yes, his microphone. According to Trump, some nefarious conspiracy took place to sabotage his weapon of mass instruction, throwing him off his game. This seems both implausible and irrelevant.

More realistically, Trump's defenders rightly point out that debate moderator Lester Holt hit Trump far harder than he hit Clinton. That's absolutely true. Holt interrupted Trump far more frequently -- although, in Holt's defense, Trump bulldozed both him and Clinton routinely. Holt asked Trump about birtherism and his Iraq war opposition and his IRS records and his mean comments about Clinton's "look," but didn't ask Clinton about the Clinton Foundation or Benghazi. And he asked her zero follow-up questions about her private email server. Holt clearly did Clinton's dirty work.

So what?

Trump has known this entire campaign that the media would target him. He said so before the debate. He had every opportunity to swivel and hit both Clinton and the media, and he failed to do so. That's on him.

This entire campaign is on him. It's nobody's fault but Trump's that he spends the morning after the debate complaining about a Miss Universe contestant gaining too much weight. It's nobody's fault but Trump's that he ignored hitting Clinton over the Clinton Foundation so he could massage his own feelings over his prior business bankruptcies.

Trump is the candidate. It's time for those who defend him to own it.

If they don't, if they keep allowing Trump to get away with excusing all of his failures by blaming somebody else, then they'll be paving the way to his defeat. Losers whine about the playing conditions and the referees. Winners change their game plans. Those who whine for Trump won't be winning for him.

How Donald Trump Became the Issue

October 5, 2016

On Tuesday night, by consensus, Republican vice presidential candidate Mike Pence wiped the floor with Democratic vice presidential candidate Tim Kaine. Kaine appeared nervous, flustered and confused; Pence appeared comfortable and in control. Pence's attacks on Hillary Clinton's corruption and policy evils were well-calibrated and hard-hitting.

There was only one problem: Kaine spent the entire evening hitting Donald Trump, and Pence spent the night attempting to treat Trump as though he was the child on the milk carton. Kaine slammed Trump's imbecilic comments over the course of the campaign, from Mexican judges to Miss Universe; Pence slapped back weakly with Clinton's "deplorables" comment, then registered for the Federal Witness Protection Program.

No wonder Trump was reportedly fighting mad at his running mate, according to CNN's John King. Pence didn't defend him. He spent the night trying to fight Clinton instead.

And that's a tactic Trump just won't stomach.

Going into the 2012 election, Republicans were looking for a candidate who could do one thing, and one thing well: place a glaring spotlight on Clinton, and leave it there. Clinton is one of the least popular major party candidates in American history. She had trouble escaping a brutal primary season with a near-octogenarian nutcase Vermont senator with no history of accomplishment other than being from the same state that produced Ben and Jerry's ice cream. And she has been facing down a federal investigation for setting up a private server in order to destroy or hide classified information.

So naturally, Republicans nominated the one man capable of drawing headlines to himself: Trump.

And he hasn't failed.

After the Democratic National Convention, he stepped directly into the media-set bear trap of the gold star Khan family. Then, in an attempt to correct course, he rightly went quiet for weeks, sticking to the teleprompter and avoiding the media.

But during the first presidential debate, Trump couldn't stop being Trump. Taunted by Clinton into defending himself over everything from IRS records to his position on the Iraq War to the aforementioned Miss Universe comment, Trump melted down. And he spent the next week melting down, allowing the media to direct all of its fire against him instead of the FBI's rigged investigation of Clinton, the continuing collapse of Clinton's Syria policy and the implosion of Obamacare. He jabbered about her cheating on Bill Clinton. And blabbed about Miss Universe's weight again and again.

Donald Trump made Election 2016 about Donald Trump.

Pence tried his best to put the genie back in the bottle during the vice presidential debate. VP debates simply don't have that kind of weight. But Pence may have given Trump a chance -- one last chance -- to reset.

And so, the question, as always, returns to Trump. Can he control himself? The Trump campaign now says that Trump will hit Clinton over her intimidation of her husband's alleged rape and sexual harassment victims. But can Trump attack in methodical fashion, or will he lose his mind when Clinton jabs him? Can Trump even stand a week of decent coverage of his running mate, whom the media will rightly characterize as a candidate focused on the 2020 or 2024 elections?

The smart money's on Trump failing. But Trump has beaten the house before. The problem is that he'll have to beat the house by folding a bad hand rather than going all in. And that's never been his strength.

The Astounding Hypocrisy of Hollywood, the Media and the Democrats on the Trump Tape

October 12, 2016

This week has been a full-scale disaster for Republican candidate Donald Trump. His poll numbers are dropping toward Australia. His establishment-Republican supporters are panicking. His campaign has swiveled toward slapping defectors rather than drawing new voters.

All of this is because Trump turned out to be a Hollywood media celebrity with Democratic leanings...who ran as a Republican.

How else could we explain the media's sudden obsession with a 2005 tape of Trump riding on an "Access Hollywood" bus? In the tape, Trump jabbers in disgusting fashion about wanting to "f---" a married woman and his tendency to "just start kissing (women)." He said: "It's like a magnet. Just kiss. I don't even wait. And when you're a star, they let you do it. You can do anything. ... Grab them by the p---y. You can do anything."

This is reprehensible. It's repulsive. It's a celebration of sexual abuse. But the left's sudden shock and dismay don't wash.

Trump said all of this on a lot in Hollywood. Here are a couple of other Hollywood names that might jog your memory: Roman Polanski and Woody Allen. Polanski earned a standing ovation at the 2003 Oscars after winning an Academy Award for "The Pianist." He was convicted of raping a 13-year-old girl both vaginally and anally in 1977. The offense happened at Jack Nicholson's home. Woody Allen's ex-wife and children still say that he sexually abused his adopted daughter when she was 7 years old. But he continues to receive plaudits and rave reviews from his friends in Tinseltown.

And the Hollywood casting couch remains alive and well. But Trump said that he engaged in precisely the same behaviors other Hollywood stars often engage in, and the Hollywoodites are up in arms.

Is it possible that's because he's a Republican?

Then there's the media. NBC had access to this tape for 11 years. A producer from "The Apprentice" claims that there are "far worse" tapes of Trump than those released by "Access Hollywood." But Trump somehow maintained a top-rated show on NBC for over a decade despite such activities, and NBC continued to play him up as a wonderful rough-and-tumble business genius. Yet MSNBC and NBC are now ripping Trump up and down for precisely the sort of behavior they overlooked when he was earning them cash.

Is it possible that's because he's a Republican?

Then there are the Democrats. They claim that Trump's comments are disqualifying. Yet they backed President Bill Clinton despite allegations of rape, sexual assault and sexual harassment; and now they back Hillary Clinton despite allegations that she has targeted her husband's victims. They lauded the late Sen. Ted Kennedy as a moral force in the Senate, despite the fact that he drove a car off a bridge with a woman in the back seat and left her to drown. They still worship at the altar of John F. Kennedy Jr., who allegedly sexually harassed interns on a grand scale. But Trump's the end of the world.

Is it possible that's because he's a Republican?

Here's the truth: Trump isn't a Republican in anything other than name. His politics are statist, and he donated more money to Democrats than Republicans between 1980 and 2010. He's a Hollywood insider, a man who appeared at the Emmy Awards alongside Megan Mullally of "Will & Grace." He's a media member, too -- NBC paid him for years. All of these groups knew what Trump was for decades. But they'll punish him because he's a Republican. That's how social standards work for the left: If you have the right politics, you can get away with anything. If you have the wrong ones, it'll ignore its own hypocrisy to nail you to the wall.

The Democratic Normal Shouldn't Be Normal

October 19, 2016

There's no question that this election cycle has seen a bevy of radical media double standards. Donald Trump's sexual harassment and assault accusers have been treated as headline news; allegations about intimidation of sexual harassment and assault victims by Hillary Clinton have been utterly ignored. Trumpian bigotry against a Mexican judge dominated the news cycle for weeks; Clinton-connected bigotry against Catholics went completely unnoticed. We heard for a full week about a Miss Universe contestant Trump allegedly called "Miss Piggy" back in 1997; we've heard very little about Hillary Clinton's perverse dealings with the media and the FBI. We've heard for months about Trump's toxic impact on politics; we've seen precious few headlines about the firebombing of a GOP campaign headquarters in North Carolina or shattered windows at other GOP operations or the repeated violent attempts to disrupt Trump rallies or hurt Trump fans.

Part of this is the allure of novelty: Trump's a new figure in politics, and every bit of information now hitting the newsstands seems fresh. Meanwhile, Clinton's been in politics for decades, which means that every allegation of corruption and nastiness merely reinforces general perceptions about her.

But there's something else afoot here: Most Americans simply expect Democrats to act like Hillary Clinton and get away with it.

Take, for example, the new allegations by James O'Keefe that Clinton-associated parties are involved in promoting voter fraud and violence at Trump rallies. O'Keefe's Project Veritas went undercover with a Democratic operative who openly admitted to encouraging people to rent cars in order to drive to precincts and vote illegally. "You use shells," said the operative. "Use shell companies. Cars come in from one company; the paychecks come from another. There's no bus involved, so you can't prove that it's en masse, so it doesn't tip people off."

The operative also admitted to attempting to provoke violence at Trump events. "You put people in the line, at the front which means that they have to get there at six in the morning because they have to get in front of the rally," he said, "so that when Trump comes down the rope line, they're the ones asking him the question in front of the reporter, because they're pre-placed there." The activist admitted that a 69-year-old woman supposedly beaten up by a Trump supporter was actually working for him. That event generated major national headlines: "Arrest warrant issued in assault of 69-year-old female protester at NC Trump rally," blared The Washington Post at the time; "69-year-old says she was 'cold-cocked' by Trump supporter during protest," said Mediaite; "Video shows aftermath of 69-year-old woman punched at a Trump rally," reported The Los Angeles Times.

None of this seems to rate national attention. Has that 69-year-old woman, Shirley Teter, appeared on national news anytime this week? Apparently not. How about the firebombing of the Trump offices? Nope. And when's the next time Hillary Clinton will be asked about her position on voter ID now that it appears some associated with her campaign have been deliberately flouting voting law?

Some of this is due to the media's leftism. But a good deal of it is due to the fact that corruption regularized over time simply becomes background noise. Nobody expects anything else from Democrats. Americans have accepted the Democratic Party as the party of voter fraud and political violence since the 1960s. They've accepted Hillary Clinton as the candidate of manipulation and corruption since the 1990s. Democratic evils are normal; Republican evils are an ever-present source of news and interest.

That's terrible for the country. All corruption should be shocking. The fact that it isn't helps explain why the 2016 election has become a competition in pursuing new lows: The old lows just don't register anymore.

An Honest Question for All Voting Americans

October 26, 2016

In 1996, "The Simpsons" did a "Treehouse of Horror" episode featuring Bill Clinton running against Bob Dole. Halfway through the episode, during a presidential debate, Homer Simpson reveals that both candidates are "hideous space reptiles," complete with dripping fangs, tentacles and one eye each: Kodos and Kang. The crowd screams in shock and horror. Then one of the aliens, Kodos, speaks: "It's true; we are aliens. But what are you going to do about it? It's a two-party system. You have to vote for one of us." The crowd mutters in stunned agreement. One fellow speaks up: "Well, I believe I'll vote for a third-party candidate!" "Go ahead," says Kang, "throw your vote away." Both aliens laugh hysterically as the crowd frets.

Welcome to election 2016.

But this election does raise a serious question for people of all political affiliations: Do the political ends justify the means? Is there *anyone* who agrees with you on policy for whom you would not vote?

The myth of the binary vote would force a "no" answer. If you must choose between two candidates, you choose the one who best reflects your policy priorities. But what if the candidate who best reflects your policy priorities is utterly unpalatable as a politician or a human being? What do you do then?

You vote for him or her anyway.

Take, as a hypothetical, a David Duke senatorial candidacy in Louisiana. A vicious racist and anti-Semite, former Ku Klux Klan head Duke is indeed running for Senate, and he's garnering some 5 percent of the vote there; he'll be included in the broadcast debate. Assume, for a moment, that Duke were the prospective 60th vote in the Senate to repeal Obamacare. Would Republicans vote for him?

Most Republicans, asked about voting for David Duke, would likely say no to his candidacy no matter the circumstances. But some wouldn't. They'd simply say that Duke on policy would be better than his Democratic opponent. Why lose a Senate seat to prove a point?

This is precisely the argument now taking place over Donald Trump on the Republican side of the aisle. No, Trump isn't David Duke, of course. But that's not the point: The argument in favor of Trump has had little to do with his qualities, and much to do with his status as the Not Hillary. That's dangerous moral territory, at best. It's basic "ends justify the means" logic. And that logic approves of *any action by a candidate* so long as that candidate votes the right way on an issue about which you care.

Conservatives used to mock such thinking. We used to scoff at Democrats calling Sen. Teddy Kennedy, D-Mass, a man who left a woman to drown in the back of his car, the "lion of the Senate." We used to sneer at the Democratic notion that Bill Clinton could get away with sexual assault so long as he backed abortion-on-demand.

Perhaps years of Democratic rule from the White House has forced Republicans to abandon the notion that character matters in the slightest; perhaps we've just decided to become Democrats of the right. If so, let's be honest about it. But let's also recognize where such voting logic leads: directly to the worst people in positions of the greatest power. Many Trump supporters are fond of saying that they'd back Stalin to stop Hitler. But that's not the question. The real question is whether they'd vote for Hitler to stop the Communist threat in 1933 Germany, or vote for the Communists to stop Hitler. After all, it was a binary choice.

Or perhaps it wasn't. Perhaps more people should have stood up and said "no" to the available choices.

If we all demanded more from our candidates, we'd get better candidates. But the binary election system creates a collective-action problem: If conservatives stand by their guns on character and Democrats don't, Democrats have an inherent political advantage.

Unless, of course, Republicans can start making the case for character, rather than adopting the belief that character simply doesn't matter. Unless Republicans forego Kodos and Kang and demand something better. If they don't, we're doomed to a lifetime of Kodos-vs.-Kang elections, all the while patting ourselves on the back that we're saving the country from the lesser of two evils.

What FBI Director Comey Did Wrong

November 2, 2016

In July, FBI Director James Comey shattered his near-sterling reputation by letting Hillary Clinton off the hook. After delivering a meticulous case against Clinton for setting up a private server and allowing classified information to flow into it illegally, he inexplicably decided not to recommend indictment by the Department of Justice.

This followed hard on President Obama announcing he would begin publicly campaigning for Clinton, Attorney General Loretta Lynch meeting secretly with Bill Clinton at a tarmac in Arizona and the FBI performing a peremptory interview with Hillary Clinton -- after which Clinton attended a late showing of "Hamilton." Minutes before Obama took the stage with Clinton, allowing her to use a lectern with the presidential seal, Comey announced there would be no indictment.

Comey's decision set off jubilation in Democratic circles, and rage in conservative ones. I wrote for National Review, "This sort of open moral debauchery would have made Boss Tweed blush."

Then came last Friday.

Comey announced, in a letter to lawmakers, that new emails had been found on a device in Anthony Weiner's possession -- no, not *that* device -- and that they could shed new light on the Clinton private server investigation. All hell broke loose. Democrats immediately labeled Comey faithless, a political hack manipulated by the Russians. Republicans said that all was forgiven and that Comey had finally correct his original error.

In reality, Comey merely committed the cardinal moral sin: He valued his institution over doing the right thing. He did it in July, and he did it again in October.

In July, Comey decided that he didn't want the FBI dragged into the presidential election. To that end, he stepped beyond the normal powers delegated to the director of the FBI and publicly requested that the DOJ not intervene with Clinton. His goal: to protect the FBI from accusations by the left of politicization. And just to demonstrate how apolitical the FBI supposedly was, Comey listed all the findings of the investigation.

The result: The left was overjoyed, and the right thought the FBI rigged.

Now, Comey wants to ensure that the FBI isn't accused of being a Hillary Clinton tool. He knew as soon as he heard about Weiner's device that he'd eventually have to tell the public about the re-initiation of the Clinton investigation, and he feared that if he waited until after the election he'd expose the FBI to a thousand Hillary-controlled-the-FBI allegations. So he came forward.

The result: The right was overjoyed, and the left thought the FBI rigged.

Whenever someone seeks to protect an institution rather than telling the truth, the institution pays the price. When NFL Commissioner Roger Goodell attempted to soft-pedal the abuse of women in the NFL in order to "protect the shield," he only ended up destroying the brand. When Chief Justice John Roberts voted to uphold Obamacare in the name of protecting the reputation of the Supreme Court, he only ended up destroying that reputation. Comey has destroyed the reputation of the FBI.

The only solution to the complete undermining of institutions lies in the honesty of those who head those institutions. At least Comey came clean this time. For Comey and the FBI, though, it's too little, too late.

Is Race Baiting Finished?

November 9, 2016

Donald Trump won the most shocking election victory in American history on Tuesday evening. He did so in the face of a media calling him racist, labeling his supporters "deplorables" and terming his victory a sign of "whitelash," as Van Jones of CNN put it. He won a higher percentage of blacks and Hispanics than Mitt Romney in 2012; Hillary Clinton drew a far lower turnout among minorities than Barack Obama.

All of this suggests that the left's race card may be dead.

It may be dead because Obama's presidency killed it.

Obama came into office on the wings of high-flown rhetoric about coming together as a nation, healing our centurieslong racial rift. Instead, he delivered a racially polarized presidency, suggesting that American law enforcement was plagued by systemic anti-black bias and that the American justice system sought to crush minorities. The despicable Black Lives Matter movement earned White House invites, and police departments earned Department of Justice consent decrees.

Mitt Romney -- perhaps the most decent man to run for the White House in the last century -- was pilloried by all of these forces as a nefarious agent of bigotry. Vice President Joe Biden said openly that Romney wanted to put black people "back in chains." Obama himself stated that Romney wanted to push America back to the 1950s -- a backhanded reference to segregation.

The media treated any and all opposition to Obama's policies as a form of covert racism; MSNBC trafficked in such nonsense for eight long years. Hosts on CNN held up their hands in the "hands up, don't shoot" posture, even though that posture itself was based on a lie. The media routinely crafted narrative lies about police-involved killings, ranging from Michael Brown to Freddie Gray, then covered the ensuing riots as "uprisings" and spontaneous outbursts of underprivileged rage against the white superstructure, even in cities with a black majority, like Baltimore, Maryland.

On college campuses, professors preached the lie of "white privilege," the concept that all racial inequalities in American society must be due to a structural imbalance created by whiteness. "Safe spaces," including racially segregated spaces, became common, even as white students were told that to say that the phrase "I'm colorblind" was a "microaggression" requiring a "trigger warning."

By the time Trump came around, the American people were sick and tired of it all. They didn't want to hear about Trump's supposedly Hitlerian tendencies -- the media had already punched itself out with Romney. They didn't want to hear from Clinton and Obama about American "deplorables" -- not after watching American cities burn with Obama's tacit approval. They didn't want to hear from diversity-oriented, six-figure-earning college professors about white privilege. They just wanted a candidate who told them they weren't a bunch of racists, that America was still a good and great place.

So the race card failed.

But it is a mistake to think it's gone forever. The demographics are still shifting. The race card is dead with white voters, but it's still very much alive with minority voters. And Democrats will not run another white person for the presidency again -- not after Clinton's dramatic failure among minorities in the wake of Obama's new minority-heavy electoral coalition. Meanwhile, Trump has an opportunity, as president, to reach out and demonstrate that the race card is a lie and a sham. Here's hoping he does it, rather than hunkering down in a bubble of his own support.

America's Celebrity Class Versus Flyover Country

November 16, 2016

On the Saturday night after Donald Trump's stunning presidential victory over Hillary Clinton, "Saturday Night Live" decided to forego its mandate -- humor -- in favor of a full-on political wake. Kate McKinnon, who has done a creditable job mocking Clinton for most of this election cycle, led off the show with a full rendition of the recently deceased Leonard Cohen's "Hallelujah." There were zero laughs and plenty of delicious, delicious celebrity tears.

McKinnon wasn't the only one crying. Lady Gaga, who introduced Clinton at her last pre-election rally, apparently wept openly backstage as Clinton lost on election night. So did Cher. Katy Perry was so overcome that she skipped singing the national anthem.

Lena Dunham of "Girls" and bragging-about-sexually-abusing-her-sister-in-her-memoir fame penned an open letter: "I touched my face and realized I was crying. 'Can we please go home?' I said to my boyfriend. I could tell he was having trouble breathing, and I could feel my chin breaking into hives. ... At home I got in the shower and began to cry even harder. My boyfriend, who had already wept, watched me as I mumbled incoherently, clutching myself."

To put it mildly, bwahahaha. Or less mildly, BWAHAHAHA.

The left spent its time during this election cycle lecturing Americans from the Hollywood Hills. It didn't work. After years of President Barack Obama traipsing into studios in Los Angeles to read mean tweets, after nearly a decade of listening to the sophomoric unearned moral superiority of actors and actresses who earn millions for reading lines other people write, after watching 9/11 truther rappers go to the White House, Americans said no to celebrity culture.

And they did so by electing a celebrity.

The great irony of Trump's victory is that he was an anti-celebrity celebrity. He had all the perks of celebrity, but he reveled in them. He didn't try to claim that he was a better human being than white middle-class voters in Wisconsin by virtue of living in New York in a penthouse covered in gold leaf. Trump played the everyman on television, and it worked.

Meanwhile, celebrities who didn't grow up in tremendous wealth hobnobbed with the elites. Singers and actresses taped a "Fight Song" rendition for the Democratic National Convention. Dunham appeared onstage at the convention. Beyonce and Jay-Z campaigned for Clinton. So did Bruce Springsteen. And all of them did so for a woman whose closest contact with flyover country came during a highly choreographed stop at Chipotle.

Americans may never get over their obsession with celebrity. But they sure don't want to hear those celebrities talk down to them. Hollywood has disconnected itself from rural America, and rural Americans were more than willing to punish Hollywood for that sin. If Democrats hope to win down the road, they'll have to do better than trotting out the scornful glitterati.

Will Conservatives Stand up to Trump if They Must?

November 23, 2016

Here's an alternate-reality scenario.

It's 2016, and the president-elect of the United States is ready to take office. Her chief advisor pledges a trillion-dollar stimulus package directed at infrastructure. The advisor explains: "It's everything related to jobs. The conservatives are going to go crazy. I'm the guy pushing a trillion-dollar infrastructure plan. ... It's the greatest opportunity to rebuild everything. Shipyards, iron works, get them all jacked up. We're just going to throw it up against the wall and see if it sticks. It will be as exciting as the 1930s. ... We'll govern for 50 years."

Meanwhile, President-elect Hillary Clinton allegedly meets with foreign business interests working to enrich her. She deploys her allies to inform ambassadors that if they patronize the Clinton Foundation, she'd appreciate it. She says that she'll divest herself of all connections to the Clinton Foundation but refuses to hand it off to any third party to handle, insisting instead that Chelsea Clinton run the place. Meanwhile, she brings Clinton into top-level diplomatic meetings without informing the press. When Vice President-elect Tim Kaine is met with protests at a public event, she takes to Twitter to castigate the attendees, demanding an apology. She goes on to criticize talk radio and Fox News for unfairness. "Equal time for us?" she asks.

This is an alternate reality. But each and every statement and event mentioned above has already happened to President-elect Donald Trump.

Trump's top advisor, Stephen Bannon, is pushing economic statism, grinning at the destruction of conservative economists. Trump met off the record with property developers Sagar and Atul Chordia, the builders of the first Trump-brand property in India, as well as developer Kalpesh Mehta, whose firm claims to be the "exclusive India representative of the Trump Organization." He sneaked Ivanka Trump into a meeting with Japanese Prime Minister Shinzo Abe. He tweeted his thoughts on the cast of "Hamilton" and the one-sided comedy of "Saturday Night Live," asking, "Equal time for us?"

The point of this exercise isn't to rip Trump. It's to point out that conservatives who rightly tore Hillary Clinton apart for pay-for-play corruption and hardcore big government leftism shouldn't grant Trump a free hand just because he leads the Republican Party. In fact, that's the biggest mistake Republicans can make.

Trump has already challenged traditional conservative standards. He's made Republicans back off their "character matters" arguments. He's forced Republicans to swallow anti-conservative heresies on economics (free trade is a negative; entitlements should be left alone), social issues (he thinks same-sex marriage should be enshrined by the Supreme Court and praises Planned Parenthood) and foreign policy (his coziness with Russia used to be taboo). Republicans did all of this to stop Hillary Clinton.

But now, Clinton has been dispatched. That means it's time for conservatives to hold Trump accountable. There's no longer any "better than Hillary" excuse making. It's time for Trump to perform.

It's too early to tell whether Trump will become a decent president. But conservatives ought to fight for something better than "not Hillary" -- or else, they can simply acknowledge that they had no real objective standards for those who seek to govern other than political convenience.

Why Does the Left Go Easy on Dictators?

November 30, 2016

When evil Cuban dictator Fidel Castro finally died last Friday, the left seemed deeply ambivalent. President Obama noted "the countless ways in which Fidel Castro altered the course of individual lives, families, and of the Cuban nation," as though Castro had been some sort of high school guidance counselor. Former President Jimmy Carter recalled all the wonderful times he spent by the sea with Castro, the sun gleaming off the waves. He said, "We remember fondly our visits with him in Cuba and his love of his country." Canadian Prime Minister Justin Trudeau -- aka handsome Bernie Sanders -- described Castro as "remarkable ... a larger than life leader who served his people for almost half a century."

Meanwhile, around the world, dictators wept in solidarity with Castro. Palestinian Authority dictator Mahmoud Abbas, who is currently in the 11th year of a four-year term in office, ordered the flags dropped to half-staff around his trashed territory. Russian dictator Vladimir Putin sent a telegram to Cuban President Raul Castro, saying, "Free and independent Cuba, which (Fidel Castro) and his allies built, became an influential member of the international community and became an inspiring example for many countries and nations." Chinese dictator Xi Jinping called Castro "a close comrade and a sincere friend," adding, "His glorious image and great achievements will be recorded in history forever."

What were Castro's great achievements? He presided over the economic destruction of one of the most quickly developing countries in Latin America; he arrested and imprisoned hundreds of thousands of dissidents; he caused the self-imposed exile of millions of Cubans; he watched and participated in the drowning of thousands of Cubans attempting to escape his prison island; he worked with mass murderer Che Guevara to murder political opponents. Castro was, simply put, one of the worst people in a century full of awful human beings.

So why did the left emerge to pay its respects this week?

Because at least Castro sought utopia.

Radical leftism believes that the quest for a utopian world, a world free of unfairness, justifies any cruelty against individuals. Individual rights are obstacles to communal greatness. The bricks of the tower of Babel will be mortared with the blood of those sacrificed on behalf of the vision. That's because the state -- which is really just an extension of "the people," who only exist en masse, never as individuals -- is the source of all rights. No rights can be violated if the state declares them defunct.

That's why the left only pays token homage to those who suffer at the hands of history's greatest monsters -- as Josef Stalin apocryphally put it, you can't make an omelet without breaking eggs. No wonder the left defended Stalin all the way until news broke in 1956 that Soviet leader Nikita Khrushchev had criticized Stalin's purges. Until then, Walter Duranty of The New York Times had whitewashed the murder of millions in the Ukrainian Holodomor -- he declared that he had seen the future, and it worked. And Hollywood even portrayed Stalin's show trials in a positive light in "Mission to Moscow." Today, Hollywood produces fawning biopics like "Che" (directed by Steven Soderbergh) and "The Motorcycle Diaries" (produced by Robert Redford), and The New York Times titled its obituary for Castro, "A Revolutionary Who Defied the U.S. And Held Cuba in His Thrall."

Dictators everywhere are safe so long as leftism reigns. And leftism will continue to reign so long as men dream of a collective heaven on Earth rather than of individual rights protected from such utopian totalitarians.

When Democracy Fails

December 7, 2016

One of the great lies of the 21st century is that republicanism and freedom are inevitable. Actually, representative government and individual liberty are the exception, not the rule, and individual liberty often dissipates in the name of the collective, along with truly representative government. And yet, it's that feeling of inevitability that allows us to attack the basic values that undergird republicanism and freedom. Because we never think that those institutions are under assault, we're unafraid of chipping away at their foundations in the name of partisan politics.

If we chip away enough at those foundations, the superstructure will crumble.

Democracy relies on three factors, as expressed by Harvard University's Yascha Mounk and the University of Melbourne's Roberto Stefan Foa: a belief that democracy is itself important, a belief that nondemocratic forms of government are wrong and a belief that the democratic system is legitimate. If those beliefs erode, so, too, do republicanism and freedom.

The left has been hammering away at those three beliefs for a full century. Leftism is based on the notion that if you give government massive power, it will revenge itself on the bourgeois who have stomped you down. More basically, Marxism is based on the notion that human beings cannot become decent without a new system. That system cannot be removed democratically, since we are all products of the democratic system, and are therefore corrupt.

Leftism, too, has scorned democracy as the only solution. Fascism of the proletariat would be better. In 2010, New York Times columnist Thomas Friedman said: "What if we could just be China for a day? I mean, just, just, just one day. You know, I mean, where we could actually, you know, authorize the right solutions, and I do think there is a sense of that, on, on everything from the economy to environment." That's not rare. The left spent most of the 1930s gazing enviously across the seas toward the fascist left in Italy, Germany and the Soviet Union.

Finally, the left has declared repeatedly that American democracy is illegitimate because it stands in favor of cruel capitalism. It's plutocratic and corrupt, and it must be heavily regulated. Today, the left claims that millions of voters are disenfranchised simply on the basis of race without evidence to support such idiocy.

But here's the problem in 2016: All three of the foundations of democracy are now being undermined by the reactionary right, too. Democracy, say many on the right, is not important so long as it means making America great again -- who cares if Carrier Corp. must be leveraged into keeping jobs at home, so long as the jobs remain at home? Democracy, say many on the right, isn't the only solution -- why not just trust Trump to do what's right? After all, he's certainly popular! And democracy doesn't work anyway, say many on the right -- the people must be lied to in order to get them to vote correctly. And voter fraud is rampant!

So we now have partisan politics that suggest that power is more important than reliable institutions or deeper values. That's a danger point for American politics. Donald Trump may turn out to be a wonderful president; we may yet see a new birth of freedom in America. But so long as partisans on both sides are prepared to blow up democracy in order to save it, we're at risk of an explosion.

'But the Democrats are Hypocrites!'

December 14, 2016

This week, the Washington Post reported that the CIA now believes that Russian-supported hacks of the Democratic National Committee and Hillary Clinton's campaign chair John Podesta were designed to boost Donald Trump's election prospects. The FBI apparently disagrees; it believes that the Russian intervention was designed to undermine faith in the election system generally. But all intelligence agencies agree that there was Russian support for the hacks themselves.

Democrats have fallen all over themselves to claim that this means that Russian President Vladimir Putin shifted the results of the election to Trump. But there's no evidence of that. Clinton was deeply unpopular for the entire election cycle -- a January 2016 YouGov/The Economist poll showed unfavorable ratings at 56 percent; in November, that same poll found her unfavorable ratings to be -- you guessed it -- 56 percent. It wasn't WikiLeaks that destroyed Hillary Clinton. It was Hillary Clinton. Even FBI Director James Comey's announcement that he would be reopening the investigation into Clinton's emails came courtesy of Anthony Weiner's laptop, not WikiLeaks.

Republicans, in response, have noted that Democrats' hysterics over Russian manipulation seems hypocritical. After all, Democrats had no problem whatsoever with President Barack Obama offering Putin "flexibility" in 2012 in exchange for a promise to loosen his pressure tactics. They cheered when Obama told Mitt Romney that he was delusional for embracing anti-Putin politics more appropriate to the 1980s. Now, Democrats are all hot and bothered about Putin's regime -- the same regime that Hillary Clinton handed a reset button, the same regime Obama allowed to take the lead in Syria, the same regime with which Obama meekly complied after Putin's takeover of Crimea.

Republicans are right: Yes, Democrats are awful hypocrites on Russia.

Here's the problem: So are Republicans. Trump questioned whether the Russians were behind the hacks at all. That's no surprise -- he spent most of the election cycle lathering up Putin's bare chest, congratulating him for his strength and equating his murder of journalists with some unspecified American sins. Trump then nominated Rex Tillerson to be secretary of state, a man who received the Order of Friendship from Putin in 2011.

So, what are Republicans doing during all of this? Capitulating. Former House Speaker Newt Gingrich calls the Tillerson pick wonderful -- the same Newt Gingrich who said in 2012 that Putin "represents a dictatorial approach that's very violent." (Of course, Gingrich now gives a lecture to the Heritage Foundation on the principles of Trumpism, so that's not much of a surprise.) Sean Hannity has accused anyone with questions about Russian hacking of simply wanting to undermine Trump. He said, "If all of these people care so much about these Russian allegations, then why didn't they feel the same way about Hillary Clinton's private server scandal?" We did! In fact, we spent years ripping Clinton apart. And now we'd like to know why Putin's hacking is all right. By the way, Hannity used to care about Russian interference and aggression. In March 2012, he called Putin a "huge problem," and in June 2013, he lamented that Putin was "laughing at the Obama admin's request to extradite Snowden back to the U.S." Now he wants Julian Assange, who is allegedly working with Putin, freed (in 2010 he wanted him jailed).

Here's the problem with the hypocrisy argument: You have to be nonhypocritical in order to make that charge. So long as Republicans are so intent on backing Trump's play that they act like hypocrites, it's going to be difficult to point out just how hypocritical Democrats are.

Obama Tries to Define Away Reality, but Reality Wins

December 21, 2016

Last Friday, President Obama gave his last press conference as commander in chief. Undeterred by his would-be successor's devastating loss to Donald Trump in the presidential election, unswayed by Republicans' complete domination of Congress, state legislatures and governor mansions, he maintained his cool and collected self-aggrandizement. Why not? According to Obama, Obama has been a major success.

Perhaps the most hilarious moment of delusion came when he talked about terrorism. "Over the past eight years, no foreign terrorist organization has successfully executed an attack on our homeland that was directed from overseas," Obama stated. He then continued, saying no attack has been executed "in a rainstorm with the attacker driving a tractor with one hand, drinking a Miller High Life with the other and wearing a clown nose."

To be fair, Obama didn't add those final qualifiers. But he might as well have. In order to define away the problem of terrorism that has grown dramatically worldwide on his watch, he simply spoke of terrorism as a problem of organized groups within defined territories. That's not how modern terrorism works. Terrorist groups can recruit without formal structures and can operate as independent cells within various countries.

Just three days after Obama's statements, an alleged jihadi plowed a truck into a Christmas market in Berlin; the same day, a Turkish terrorist murdered the Russian ambassador to Turkey. These latest attacks aren't outliers. In the past several years, we've seen terrorist attacks in Turkey, Germany, Belgium, Great Britain, Canada and Australia.

This sort of terrorism isn't relegated to foreign countries, of course. Here is an incomplete list of radical Islam-related terror attacks and attempts on American soil under Obama: shootings of American military recruiters in Little Rock, Arkansas; the massacre at Fort Hood; the Boston Marathon bombing; an attempted bombing of the airport in Wichita, Kansas; hatchet attacks on New York City police officers; attempted shootings at the "Draw Muhammad" event in Garland, Texas; the attacks on military recruiters in Chattanooga, Tennessee; the massacre at the San Bernardino Inland Regional Center; the Orlando nightclub shooting; the New York and New Jersey bombings; and the Ohio State University car attack.

Obama still thinks he can cover his abysmal record with closely drawn definitions of terrorism. It's the equivalent of President Bill Clinton saying he's been faithful to his wife except for certain areas, like sex. It's technically true so far as it goes, but it doesn't go very far.

Americans know that, and they reacted to Obama's consistent lying-by-omission by electing Trump, a man who needs little evidence to jump to conclusions. Obama is so careful to avoid spotting fact patterns that he simply omits inconvenient data points. Trump is so eager to spot fact patterns that he simply includes convenient non-data points. But Americans would rather have Trump's jump-to-conclusions mentality than Obama's avoid-conclusions-at-all-cost mentality -- Trump's mentality may lead to mistakes, but those mistakes are less likely to cost Western lives.

So Obama can hawk his faux sophistication on terrorism as much as he wants. If Democrats want to ensure that Republicans continue to win elections, they ought to follow his lead.

Obama's Skewed Moral Universe

December 28, 2016

President Barack Obama likes to see himself as a moral leader. "The arc of the moral universe is long," Obama likes to say, quoting Martin Luther King Jr, "but it bends toward justice." According to Obama, Obama is a genteel representative of decency and good grace, a man pointing America toward a broader vision, a fellow questing for social justice and contextual consideration.

In reality, he's a narcissistic fool. And like Burgess Meredith's character in "The Twilight Zone," he will be left standing in the ruins, bewailing the fates that abandoned him, leaving no worshipful admirers upon whom to lean.

Obama's legacy is one of failure all around the world. He leaves office with a genocide in Syria on his record -- a genocide he pledged to prevent, then tolerated and finally lamented, mourning the fates while blithely ignoring his own cowardice. Libya, meanwhile, remains a full-scale disaster area, with tens of thousands of refugees from that failed campaign swamping Europe, along with those fleeing Syria, and his leftist European allies paying the political price.

Iran, the world's leading state sponsor of terrorism, stands on the brink of a nuclear dawn, its pockets filled with billions of dollars, its minions ascendant from Tehran to Aleppo to Beirut. Obama made that happen with nearly a decade of appeasement and a willingness to abandon freedom-minded Iranians to the tender mercies of the mullahs.

Meanwhile, Russia has only expanded its reach and influence, invading the sovereign nation of Ukraine and seizing Crimea to the deafening silence of the Obama administration. Russia has flexed its muscle in Kaliningrad, where it has stocked missiles, and in Syria, where it has assured Syrian President Bashar Assad's continued dominance.

China has grown its sphere of influence across the South China Sea, putting American allies from Taiwan and Japan to the Philippines directly under its thumb. Thanks to Obama's military cuts, China believes that it can bully American allies into embracing Chinese supremacy in international waters -- and it may be right. Simultaneously, Obama continues to drive America into debt, and the Chinese are large buyers of that outstanding debt.

The communist Cubans have been re-enshrined; so have the socialist Venezuelan authorities. The Islamic State group remains an international threat, and western capitals have been struck by Islamic terror time and again, to Obama's teeth-gnashing and general inaction.

But at least Obama is truly putting his focus where it's necessary: on declaring that our only ally in the Middle East, Israel, has no historic claim to its own existence and threatening Jews with sanctions for building bathrooms in East Jerusalem.

Obama came into office amidst grand promises to restore America's place in the world. Unless our place is the outhouse, he's failed. But at least he feels good about his accomplishments, even if thousands have died -- and thousands more will die -- in order to ensure his moral stature in his own mind.

About the Author

Ben Shapiro was born in 1984. He entered the University of California Los Angeles at the age of 16 and graduated summa cum laude and Phi Beta Kappa in June 2004 with a Bachelor of Arts degree in Political Science. He graduated Harvard Law School cum laude in June 2007.

Shapiro was hired by Creators Syndicate at age 17 to become the youngest nationally syndicated columnist in the United States. His columns are printed in major newspapers and websites including *The Riverside Press-Enterprise* and the *Conservative Chronicle*, Townhall.com, ABCNews.com, WorldNetDaily.com, Human Events, FrontPageMag.com, and FamilySecurityMatters.com. His columns have appeared in *The Christian Science Monitor, Chicago Sun-Times, Orlando Sentinel, The Honolulu Advertiser, The Arizona Republic, Claremont Review of Books,* and RealClearPolitics.com. He has been the subject of articles by *The Wall Street Journal, The New York Times,* The Associated Press, and *The Christian Science Monitor.* He has been quoted on "The Rush Limbaugh Show" and "The Dr. Laura Show," at CBSNews.com, and in the *New York Press, The Washington Times,* and *The American Conservative.*

Shapiro is the author of best-sellers "Brainwashed: How Universities Indoctrinate America's Youth," "Porn Generation: How Social Liberalism Is Corrupting Our Future," and "Project President: Bad Hair and Botox on the Road to the White House." He has appeared on hundreds of television and radio shows around the nation, including "The O'Reilly Factor," "Fox and Friends," "In the Money," "DaySide with Linda Vester," "Scarborough Country," "The Dennis Miller Show," "Fox News Live," "Glenn Beck Show," "Your World with Neil Cavuto," "700 Club," "The Laura Ingraham Show," "The Michael Medved Show," "The G. Gordon Liddy

Show," "The Rusty Humphries Show," "The Lars Larson Show," "The Larry Elder Show," The Hugh Hewitt Show," and "The Dennis Prager Show."

Shapiro is married and runs Benjamin Shapiro Legal Consulting in Los Angeles.

~~~

THE ESTABLISHMENT IS DEAD
is also available as an e-book
for Kindle, Amazon Fire, iPad, Nook and
Android e-readers. Visit
creatorspublishing.com to learn more.

o o o

CREATORS PUBLISHING

We publish books.
We find compelling storytellers and
help them craft their narrative,
distributing their novels and collections
worldwide.

o o o

Made in the USA
Middletown, DE
28 March 2019